Troubleshooting Your Handgun

By
J. B. Wood

DBI BOOKS, INC./NORTHFIELD, ILLINOIS

STAFF

EDITOR
Robert S. L. Anderson

ART DIRECTION
MacDonald-Ball Studio

PRODUCTION MANAGER
Pamela J. Johnson

ASSOCIATE PUBLISHER
Sheldon L. Factor

This book is dedicated to my father, James W. Wood

Acknowledgements

In putting together this book, I received assistance from many different sources. I would like to express my appreciation to each of those who helped:

Tom Cook, Daniel M. Byrne, Steve Robbins, Archie Riehl, Bob Paschal, Bob Taylor, K. R. Jones, Glenn Lancaster, W. Paul Torrington, Bob Gunther, Ron Lankford, Larry McClarney, Jim D. Redding, J. P. Bradford, Eric Brooker, Chick Evans, Rolan Bennett, Jan Borjesson, James B. Stewart, Curt Ball, Bengt Ericsson, Thomas A. Smith, Dr. William B. Challman, James R. Harris, Terah L. Flaherty, Gene Wilson, Jan A. Stevenson, Donald M. Simmons, Jr., Dennis Riordan, and B&S Sporting Guns.

J. B. W.

ISBN 0695-80944-X

Library of Congress Catalog Card Number 78-52053

Introduction

Longtime readers of the monthly firearms publications may remember my Troubleshooting column which appeared in most issues of the late lamented *Gunfacts* magazine, and subsequently ran for around two years in *Guns & Ammo.* More recently, it has also made brief appearances in *Gun World, Gun Digest,* and *The American Handgunner.* All of the original columns appear in this book; however, most of the guns herein were not previously covered, and this material is entirely new.

This is not intended to be a handbook for the amateur gunsmith. In fact, you will often find the suggestion that you obtain the services of a competent professional gunsmith—and yes, I know how difficult that may be, in some areas. This seems to be the age of the "parts replacer" and the "specialist," with nothing in between. The old-time general gunsmith has become almost extinct. Fortunately, there are still a few left.

Throughout this book you will find references to the relative fragility of flat springs, also called "blade" or "leaf" type springs. Most modern guns principally use round-wire springs, either in helical coil or shaped otherwise according to function. It should be noted, however, that flat springs are not inherently fragile. Their tendency toward breakage depends directly on the degree to which they are flexed in normal operation. A blade-type spring not flexed to its limit may last as long as one of round wire.

The concept of *troubleshooting* is a simple one: Even the best designs are, in some areas, a compromise. Even the best designs may have a point or two that can cause trouble. It has not been my intention to imply that because of some small quirk, the subject gun is a poor one. Some of the trouble spots occur very infrequently, and these are so noted. Among the guns covered are several which I own and use regularly—the Walther PPK/S, Smith & Wesson Model 59 and others. If I thought they were mechanically deficient, I would not be using them.

To the dealer, trader, collector, shooter, or beginning gunsmith, I say this: On the gun you might own or consider buying, these things may never happen. However, here's what to watch for, and if it happens, here's what to do about it.

J. B. Wood
Raintree House
Corydon, Kentucky
October, 1977

In regard to the mechanical and safety aspects of the pistols covered in this book, it is assumed that the guns are in factory original condition with the dimensions of all parts as made by the manufacturer. Since alteration of parts is a simple matter, the reader is strongly advised to have any gun checked by a competent gunsmith. Both the author and publisher disclaim responsibility for any accidents.

Table of Contents

For an alphabetical listing of the firearms covered in TROUBLESHOOTING YOUR HANDGUN you may refer to the Alphabetical Index found on page 192.

Walther P-38 Pistol

The big Walther was the first true double-action pistol in 9mm Parabellum chambering to reach full-production status. For quite a few years, until the S&W Model 39, it was the only 9mm with double-action available. The late standard side arm of the Wehrmacht, it returned after the war and is now available in commercial form. It should be pointed out that the remarks which follow refer to the common wartime issue P-38, as the postwar model was slightly redesigned, and some of these points do not apply.

In the smaller PP, PPK, and PPK/S pistols, the safety shields the firing pin head when applied. In the P-38, the safety lever rolls twin shoulders on the safety drum upward to contact opposing surfaces on the body of the firing pin, blocking its travel. The two shoulders on the safety are each only about $\frac{1}{16}$-inch wide, with a maximum depth of $\frac{3}{32}$-inch. Like the smaller Walthers, the P-38 also has the automatic hammer-drop when the safety is used, one of Herr Walther's least inspired innovations. Considering this, and the possibility of metal fatigue from repeated impact on those relatively narrow shoulders, the P-38 safety is less sure than those of the smaller pistols. If the pistol has a full magazine when the safety is applied and breakage occurs, the effect can be quite unsettling—the hammer-drop system will keep it going until the magazine is empty. I have in my files a hilarious letter (though I'm sure he wasn't amused at the time) from a gentleman who had to buy a new tailgate for his brother-in-law's pickup truck, after an ailing P-38 ran amok across it.

If you do much shooting with a P-38, have a qualified gunsmith check the impact surfaces of firing pin and safety drum. While you're at it, have him remove the hammer-drop lever from the frame. Then, to be doubly safe, use both hands to let the hammer down gently, after the safety is applied.

The big Walther has one other quirk. Over the years, I have become accustomed to a familiar sight—the unhappy shooter with a "topless" P-38. The more fortunate ones also bring a few of the parts they've managed to find in the tall grass. The P-38 slide top cover, which also retains the rear sight, is held at the rear by twin projections which hook solidly under a shelf inside the slide. At the front, however, the retention is not as solid. Two forward projec-

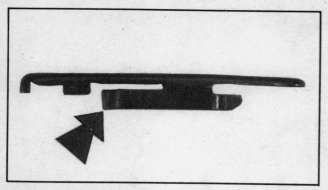

Lack of proper tension on the forward locking arms (arrow) of the slide top cover can result in the cover being blown off during shooting.

When the slide top cover is blown off, these are the parts you'll go scrambling for: the cover, firing pin retainer, firing pin lock and spring, plus the rear sight. Be sure the cover fits—properly.

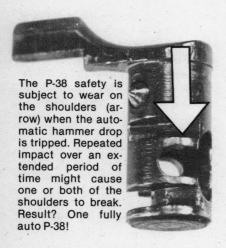

The P-38 safety is subject to wear on the shoulders (arrow) when the automatic hammer drop is tripped. Repeated impact over an extended period of time might cause one or both of the shoulders to break. Result? One fully auto P-38!

tions are spring-tempered and at their side edges snap under very narrow ledges inside the slide. When the spring tension of these arms weakens, or their locking edges in the slide become less sharp, even the low-powered standard U.S. commercial round can cause the top cover to depart. With one of the hotter 9mm loadings, it becomes even more likely. When it happens, the shooter can usually find the top cover, but smaller parts such as the rear sight, firing pin retainer, and automatic firing pin lock and spring are often gone forever.

To lessen the chances of this, have a gunsmith check the tension of the spring arms on the top cover, reshaping them outward, if necessary. It is also possible to deepen the retaining ledges inside the slide, but this will make future disassembly more difficult.

At this time, the replacement parts situation for the P-38 is not critical. Many of the used-parts dealers still have a good supply, and currently-made replacement firing pins are available from several sources. Springs and small parts, such as the firing pin retainer, can be made by a gunsmith. It should be noted that several of the parts for the postwar pistol, available from the importer, Interarms, will not interchange with those of the wartime P-38.

Walther PP, PPK and PPK/S Pistols

The Walther PP, as pictured above is an early wartime production model. The "PP" designation stands for "Police Pistol."

Everyone who has read a little about the Walther pistols knows that the Modell PP first appeared in 1929, while the smaller PPK didn't arrive until two years later, in 1931, right? Wrong. Recently discovered data has shown that the first PPK was made later in the same year as the larger pistol, 1929. For a while there, they weren't even sure what to call it. Very early examples, while PPK in every detail, were marked "Modell PP." In a short time, though, Walther decided that if the larger one was the Polizei Pistole (Police Pistol), the reduced-size version should be the Polizei Pistole Kriminal, since the Police Detective force in Germany is called the Kriminal Polizei. Now, let's move forward in time to 1968 when our own wise leaders decided that a pistol 1/10-inch less in height than their magic numbers could only be used for criminal purposes and banned the PPK from importation. The Walther people were equal to the challenge. They simply mated a PPK slide and barrel to a PP frame and gave us the PPK/S —the "S" standing for "Spezial," which requires no translation. One of these, wearing cocobolo custom grips by Jean St. Henri and loaded with eight .380 hollow-points, is ly-ing in the desk drawer near my right elbow as I write this. Enough of this background stuff—let's examine the pistols.

When you see the Walther "banner" trademark, you know the gun is made of the finest materials, with fit and finish that must have been done in the Black Forest by quality-conscious elves. In the .380 chambering, where many other pistols have to visit the gunsmith for "throating" to handle the hollow-points and other bullets of nonstandard shape, the Walther, just as it comes from the factory at Ulm on the Donau, will function with anything. Also, for a pocket pistol, it's extremely accurate. Hardly anything ever goes wrong. Nevertheless, over the years I have repaired a few.

Let's concentrate first on the safety system. When the safety lever is in "fire" position, its pivot-drum presents a concave surface to the hammer, exposing the head of the firing pin. When the lever is moved to "safe," the drum rolls a convex surface up to shield the head of the firing pin, while internal shoulders block any forward movement. So far, a good system.

Unfortunately, however, Walther added a sear-trip at the end of the safety-lever travel. The safety

This particular Walther is a true PPK (Polizei Pistole Kriminal) as made prior to WW II. The frame on this gun is slightly shorter than the PP or PPK/S. The PP, PPK/S and PPK will be found chambered for either the .32 or .380 ACP.

Walther's PPK/S represents a marriage of the PP frame and the PPK slide. The PPK/S was specifically designed to meet the importation "point-system" resulting from the GCA of '68.

drum, the round pivot which crosses inside the slide, is extensively skeletonized for the firing pin—the concave cut for firing position—and the locking shoulder. The two ends of the drum are connected only by a pair of relatively narrow bridges of steel. With the safety in firing position, the concave face of the drum will distribute the impact of the hammer over an area about ¼-inch square. In the "safe" position, however, the sear-trip drops the hammer on a rounded surface, concentrating the impact on a very narrow line across the rounded surface of the drum. Over a period of years, this repeated impact can crack one or both of the cross-bridges. I have replaced several safety levers that were broken in this manner and rejoined quite a few others with weld or silver solder. There is one good point—if it should happen to your pistol, the gun is not likely to accidentally fire, as all of the parts are still firmly supported, even if broken.

There are two ways to make this sort of breakage unlikely. When the hammer is cocked, and you operate the safety, always ease the hammer down gently with the thumb of the other hand. Another way is to simply have a gunsmith remove the sear-trip from the pistol so that the hammer will not automatically fall when the safety is applied. My own PPK/S has this alteration.

An occasional source of difficulty is the cartridge indicator pin. As a cartridge is chambered, its rim pushes the forward end of the indicator upward. As the slide closes, the indicator strikes the upper rear face of the barrel and is pushed toward the rear, where its tip protrudes just above the hammer to show that there is a car-

The safety of the PP, PPK/S and PPK has two narrow connecting bridges which are subject to some degree of pounding over an extended period of use. When the safety is tripped, the hammer falls hard—a cracked bridge or bridges may result with years of hard use.

tridge in the chamber. The indicator must have spring pressure both forward and downward, and any tension variation in its single little spring, or a slight bend in the indicator, can jam the system. If it is jammed in the down and forward position, it can cause misfeeding. If it's jammed to the rear, it will falsely indicate a cartridge in the chamber. Any of these things can be corrected by reshaping or replacing the spring or the indicator.

As many owners of the Walther PP, PPK, and PPK/S will know, 99 percent of these pistols will never have any of the problems outlined above. From the late unlamented Gestapo to the legendary James Bond, for the off-duty policeman or the private citizen protecting his family, the Walther has always been and will continue to be a good choice.

Walther Model 4 Pistol

(Above) This Walther Model 4 is of later manufacture. It has an internal trigger bar.

The fourth in the Walther line, this 7.65mm (.32 auto) pistol was made from 1910 to 1918. During this time, it underwent one slight re-design, making two distinct types for collectors to consider. The early guns had very wide slide serrations, an external trigger bar, and concentric rings on the head of the safety lever. Later guns had an increased number of narrow slide serrations, an internal trigger bar, and a checkered safety-lever head. Both types shared one unusual feature—the ejection port is on the left side of the slide.

While the Model 4 will not compare with later pistols by Walther, it had several points in the design that were worthy of note, especially when we remember the time in which it was produced. The gun has a very simple firing system, and a pivoting internal hammer. The recoil spring surrounds the barrel, giving the pistol a low vertical profile. The barrel is fixed solidly to the frame. The manual safety directly blocks both the sear and hammer.

The hammer spring is a flat blade-type, bearing on a roller at the lower front of the hammer. This spring is a relatively heavy one, and is not flexed very far when the hammer is cocked. They

rarely break. All other springs are round wire, either helical coil or torsion type. The only example of the latter is the trigger bar/disconnector spring which coils around the hammer pivot on the left side of the frame, its rear projection also serving as a positioning spring for the safety lever. The forward arm of this spring contacts a groove in the lower edge of the trigger bar to supply upward tension. It is possible, through insertion of a damaged magazine or careless disassembly, to deform the spring and cause it to lack proper alignment with its groove in the bar. This is easily corrected, and in the event that it breaks during re-shaping, making a new one is not difficult.

This is a rear-end view of the barrel sleeve which can jam the slide if deformed. In reassembly, it must go to the rear.

Occasionally the trigger bar spring (arrow) becomes misaligned from its groove at the lower edge of the bar. Misalignment is usually due to the insertion of a damaged magazine or careless disassembly.

At its rear terminus, the recoil spring enters a sleeve which serves a dual purpose. In addition to covering the spring so it is not visible and open to external dirt through the ejection port, the sleeve is the key to the takedown system, preventing the slide from rising out of its frame tracks for disassembly until the front extension, recoil spring, and sleeve are removed. The sleeve is fairly sturdy, but its thickness is limited by the internal dimensions of the slide, and if it becomes deformed, it can jam the slide. This will not happen in normal operation, but amateur reassembly sometimes puts the sleeve at the muzzle end, and if the gun is fired in this condition, damage is possible. A deformed sleeve can be restored to shape, but this requires special forming tools which the average gunsmith usually will not have on hand.

The original grips are of black molded hard rubber, and age makes them brittle. The left grip is centrally unsupported. Unfortunately, these grips are not among those which have been commercially reproduced, so when they're broken, replacements must be handmade.

On the backstrap of the grip frame is a small screw which regulates the tension of the hammer spring. If a Model 4 begins to misfire, with light firing pin dents in the cartridge primer, check to see if this screw has been loosened.

Hard rubber becomes brittle with age, and the left grip of the Model 4 is centrally unsupported—note the cracks beginning at the lower edge (arrows).

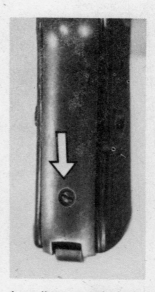

A small screw on the lower backstrap of the Model 4 regulates the tension of the hammer spring. If the screw becomes too loose, the hammer impact will be lightened, and the pistol will misfire.

Wiener "Little Tom" Pistols

(Above) The Wiener "Little Tom" pistols, in .32 and .25 caliber.

The first, regular production, double-action pocket pistol was not made by Walther. It was designed in 1908 by Alois Tomiska of Pilsen, Czechoslovakia, and was called the "Little Tom" in honor of the inventor, a direct translation of his last name. Production of the pistol was licensed in 1910 to the Wiener Waffenfabrik in Vienna, and this factory made the guns until around 1924. From 1925 to 1929, the inventor made the last of the "Little Tom" pistols himself at his small factory in Pilsen. The gun was first offered in 6.35mm (.25 auto) and was later made in a larger 7.65mm (.32 auto) version.

The double-action system of the pistol is unusual in one respect. When the hammer is cocked for single-action firing, the trigger is not retracted to the rear. The trigger must be moved from its forward double-action position back to the single-action let-off point before firing. The long bar which connects hammer and trigger is pivot-attached to the hammer with a slip-off hook for double-action at its forward end. On the underside of this bar is a beak which engages a fixed step on the frame, acting as the single-action sear—a very unique and ingenious arrangement. In single-action firing, a lever on the trigger simply pushes the bar upward, disengaging its beak from the frame detent. The only repair I've ever done to this system is to recut and sharpen the single-action engagement surfaces where wear has rounded them off. No breakage has been seen. Above the connecting bar is its spring, one of the two blade-types used in the gun. It is stake-mounted on the frame and is not severely flexed, in operation. If one should ever break, making a replacement would be very easy.

Magazine can be inserted from the bottom of the grip, but the pistol was designed to be loaded this way, locking the slide open and dropping it in from the top.

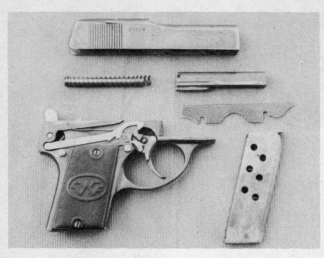

In this right side field-stripped view, the cover plate has also been removed to show the trigger, connecting bar, and its spring.

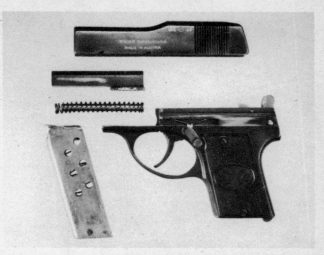

The .25 pistol, field-stripped, left side. Note the safety positioning spring, just above the safety lever.

The other flat spring is on the opposite side of the gun, a shallow V-shaped part which supplies tension for the positioning of the safety lever. The preceding remarks on the connecting bar spring also apply here. The molded hard-rubber grips are retained by two screws on each side, and on the .25 pistol the lower screw is very near the edge, making chipping in that area not unusual. Most of the .32 pistols and a few of the .25s have grips of smooth wood, and these do not break often. No commercial replacements are available.

Nearly all of these guns have magazine bodies made of brass, and there is no floorplate extension toward the front. To load the gun, a filled magazine is dropped in from the top with the slide locked open by the safety lever. There is a conventional magazine release at the lower rear of the grip frame, and the magazine can be inserted from the bottom in the usual fashion, but the factory-intended method is much easier. To remove the magazine, the slide is locked open, the pistol turned upside down, and pressing the magazine release will drop the magazine out the top into the hand. It might be expected that these brass magazines would be somewhat more susceptible to deformation, but this has not proved to be true. They are well-made, and the brass was apparently hardened after forming.

It has been said that the "Little Tom" pistols greatly influenced Fritz Walther in his design of the PP and PPK pistols. Except for the concept of double-action in a small pocket pistol, the internal design is not similar at all, so this point is debatable. One thing is very certain—it is no coincidence that manufacture of the "Little Tom" ceased in 1929, the same year that the most excellent Walther pistols appeared.

In this view, the hammer is cocked for single-action firing. The left arrow points to the engagement of the bar with the fixed sear on the frame. The right arrow indicates the sear lever/disconnector on the trigger:

In this view, the firing mechanism is at rest, ready for a double-action pull. The arrow points to the engagement of the connecting bar with the lobe of the trigger.

Jäger Pistol

The small factory of Franz Jäger in Suhl, Germany, began operations in 1901 and soon established a reputation for producing sporting arms of excellent quality. At the beginning of WW I, all German arms makers were ordered by the government to produce only guns suitable for military use. Since none of Herr Jäger's sporting arms fell into this category, he was faced with the unpleasant possibility of a complete shutdown. Instead, he quickly came up with a remarkable little 7.65mm (.32 auto) pistol which required a minimum of intricate machine work and was in fact the first handgun to use sheet-steel stampings in the production of the frame.

The Jäger Pistole employs two plates of about ³⁄₃₂-inch thickness to enclose the barrel and form the grip frame. A forward sub-frame, between the plates, includes the trigger and trigger guard and forms the frontstrap of the grip frame. The rear sub-frame houses the safety lever, sear, magazine catch and their springs. Within the slide, a separate breech block is retained by a deep groove which contacts a large cross-pin. Throughout the design there are numerous other manufacturing shortcuts in which major parts are pinned and

The ejector (arrow), is the only part in the Jäger which causes occasional difficulty.

staked in place. Considering this, you might expect that in time, after long use, the entire gun would begin to loosen up. The design is so well-engineered, though, that this doesn't happen. I have never examined one of these guns that wasn't as tight as the day it left Suhl.

There are several flat springs in this design, but as none are severely flexed, breakage is not common. It might also be noted that most of these springs are of somewhat heavier stock than normally used in pistols, and this fact doubtless adds to their long life. The only actual damage I've seen on these guns is occasional breakage of the molded hard-rubber grips, hammer marks where someone attempted to drive out the barrel positioning studs, and stripping of the ejector screw.

The ejector is a simple piece of angled sheet steel, secured to the inside of the left frame plate by a very short shallow-headed screw. Since the ejector receives a good deal of impact from the head of the cartridge case during recoil, this screw will occasionally loosen, and anyone who tightens it must remember that its threads are not extensive. A replacement can be made (there are *no* parts avail-

Arrows point to the takedown latches and to the nose on the magazine floorplate designed to operate them.

In this view, the takedown latches have been released, and the two sub-frames pivoted outward.

able), but if the threads in the frame plate are stripped, the hole will have to be re-tapped to the next larger diameter.

The Jäger pistol was made only in 7.65mm and only in blue finish. It was made for only three years, from 1914 to 1917, and in that time only about 15,000 of them were produced. Although the gun is quite reliable, it is of more interest to collectors than shooters. Franz Jäger's son, Paul Jaeger, is located in Jenkintown, Pennsylvania, and his firm is highly respected as a supplier of fine custom-built rifles.

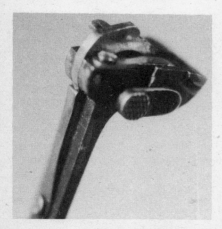

A close view of the rear sub-frame unit which houses the sear, safety lever, magazine catch, and their attendant springs. Note that the springs are of fairly heavy stock.

The Jäger pistol, disassembled. Sub-frame parts and breech block parts are still in place.

Steyr Model 1908 Pistol

This beautifully made pocket pistol was designed and patented in 1905 and 1906 by Nicolas Pieper of Herstal, Belgium, and manufacturing rights were licensed to the Oesterreichische Waffenfabrik Gesellschaft of Steyr, Austria. Manufacturing began in 1908, and the guns were put on the market in 1909. During their time of manufacture, there were three minor revisions of the design. Very early pistols have an internal breech block, enclosed by the frame except for a small portion of its top where a hump at the rear contained the rear sight and had side serrations for cocking. In the very early guns, the serrations are slanted. In later ones, they are vertical. Also, the serrated "wings" at the rear of the barrel were lengthened downward to reach the frame.

At some point in the production, a third type was also made, having a larger, heavier breech block which was not contained in the frame, but was more like a conventional slide with serrations at the lower rear sides. On this gun, an extractor was also added. Earlier types had relied on the low residual pressures of the .32 auto cartridge to blow the fired case out of the chamber.

There are several interesting features in this design. Pushing down a lever on the left side releases the barrel to tip down, exposing the chamber and disconnecting the recoil spring hook from the breech block. The original magazines have a double retaining notch, making it possible to employ the tip-open barrel in single-shot fashion, while keeping a full magazine in reserve. The hinged barrel also makes it unnecessary to cycle the slide by hand, as the last round can be dropped into the chamber, and the barrel snapped back into place.

The manual safety is particularly positive, as it directly locks the hammer. Grips are of black hard rubber on most guns with the Steyr emblem at center. On some guns, they are of checkered walnut with no emblem. Each grip is well mounted with two screws, and while they are centrally unsupported, breakage is not too common. With the molded type, some chipping at the corners is frequently found. This is not one of the grips that has been commercially reproduced, so any replacements would have to be handmade.

The disconnector system is an odd design. While most disconnectors are pushed downward by the recoiling slide or breech block, this

This Steyr Model 1908 pistol is the 7.65mm version, the type with the heavier external breech block.

Arrow points to the V-type flat spring which tips the barrel upward. On this example, the tip of its lower arm is broken off.

The trigger bar (upper arrow) and the magazine catch (lower arrow) are tempered to be their own springs. Note the thinness of both. In spite of this, they rarely break.

one is a small lever actuated by the movement of the hammer spring plunger. It works perfectly and is less susceptible to wear than the usual type.

There are several blade-type springs in the 1908 Steyr, and the one that breaks most often is the V-shaped one that tips the barrel upward. The trigger bar is also tempered to be its own spring, and where it crosses the magazine well, it is of very thin construction. When this one breaks, you are in real trouble, as there are practically no parts available, and making this one is both difficult and expensive. Fortunately, these do not often break. The same can be said for the magazine catch. If any of the other flat springs break, it is possible to replace it with doubled round wire.

In addition to the 7.65mm (.32 auto) version, the 1908 Steyr was also made in 6.35mm (.25 auto) in a reduced size. Pieper, the designer, also made a considerably modified version under his own name in Belgium.

In this view, the barrel is tipped open and the breech block is retracted. The left arrow points to the barrel latch lever. The right one indicates the manual safety lever.

Ortgies Pocket Automatic

Note the discoloration on these original Ortgies grips. It comes from an unsuccessful attempt to glue them directly to the frame. The arrow points to the retaining well which has chipped out, making the grips useless. Fortunately, plastic replacements are available.

The initial prototype of this pistol was probably made in Belgium around 1916, while Heinrich Ortgies was a resident of Liege. Some three years later, after perfecting his design, he moved to Erfurt, Germany, where he set up a manufacturing firm, and the Ortgies Pocket Automatic was born. In many ways it was a remarkable design. There are no screws at all in the gun and only four pins. The disconnector works across the frame, rather than by vertical depression. The barrel is rigidly mounted, but can be removed without tools. The gun has a very smooth exterior with no sharp projections to snag on the pocket. After only a year of manufacturing, Herr Ortgies sold the rights to make his pistol to the Deutsche Werke in Erfurt, and they continued production until around 1926. Most of the pistols were made in 7.65mm (.32 auto) and in 6.35mm (.25 auto), with a smaller number in 9mm kurz (.380 auto).

The Ortgies is a nice-looking pistol and was well-made of good materials. Unfortunately, there were several inherent weaknesses in the original design. This is a true hammerless pistol with a hollow striker mounted in the slide. In most pistols of this type, the striker is a simple hollow cylinder with a firing pin at the front and a small projection at the rear to contact the sear. In the Ortgies, the striker is of unusual design. Two long arms extend downward from the rear of the hollow tube, only one of which engages the sear. The other arm has a small side projection which runs in a track inside the slide. On the underside, between the arms, a slot extends forward ½-inch to admit the striker spring base, an extension of the grip safety. Because of the rather thin-walled construction of the striker, and the slot, and the length of the arms, breakage is frequent. When the left arm breaks, the result is immediately known, as this is the sear-contact arm. When the right arm breaks, however, allowing the striker to rotate, the trouble may not be consistent, setting the scene for an accident.

If you shoot an Ortgies with any regularity, the striker should be inspected frequently for signs of incipient fracture. Fortunately, this is one of the parts that has been reproduced commercially in recent years, and it is available from several sources.

Another common ailment concerns the interesting little discon-

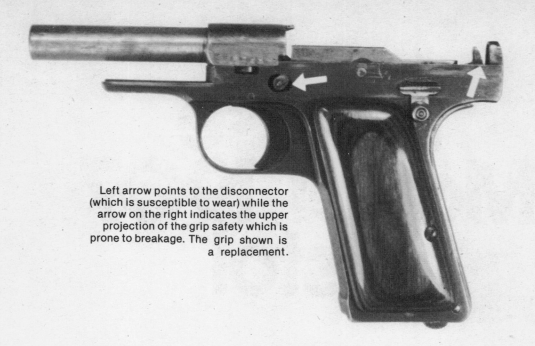

Left arrow points to the disconnector (which is susceptible to wear) while the arrow on the right indicates the upper projection of the grip safety which is prone to breakage. The grip shown is a replacement.

nector. The usual type is pushed down by the slide movement with an ample operational allowance for wear. In the Ortgies, the disconnector is a lateral-traveling button at the foward end of the sear, just above the trigger, and is depressed toward the right by the slide movement. This action disengages a thin flange on the disconnector from an equally narrow projection on the top of the trigger. The engagement is so delicate that a very small amount of wear on the slide contact surface of the button can cause the disconnector to cease functioning. The gun will not, however, go full auto, as the next round will jam on the point of the firing pin. Depending on the degree of wear, this problem can be cured by either recutting the disconnector flange or by making a new button—neither is difficult.

With the exception of one variation in the .380 version which has a manual safety lever, the only safety provided is a grip-type, and this one, too, is unusual. It snaps out to perform its function only when released by a small button just behind the top of the left grip. The grip safety blocks the sear and is powered by the striker spring. The projection which extends from the safety to contact the spring fol-

lower is also prone to breakage. In this case, the only remedy is to rejoin the broken projection to the grip safety piece using steel weld or silver solder, unless one of the used-parts dealers happens to have an Ortgies safety.

Finally, the wooden grips are attached by a spring-powered part which extends a thin projection into a recess at the inside rear of each grip panel, the grips being undercut at the forward edge. When the recesses break out—and you'll notice I said when, not if—the grips will fall off, and there is no easy way to reattach them. Plastic replacements are available, and these might last a bit longer.

As you might have gathered by now, the Ortgies is not one of the best.

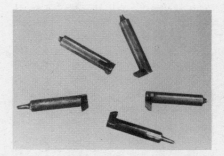

In the Ortgies design, the weakest point is the striker (firing pin). Here's an assortment, broken in various ways.

The two projections and the guide lug at the rear of this Ortgies striker are unbroken. When the lug on the left breaks, the problem is immediately apparent as it serves as the sear-contact arm. When the right lug breaks, the striker can rotate, creating inconsistent problems that can set the scene for an accident.

When the lower projections (lugs) of the striker are unbroken, it is possible to replace a broken striker point in several ways. This one was repaired by making a solid point, cutting off the striker body, and cross-pinning the point in place.

Dreyse Model 1907 Pistol

This odd-looking pocket automatic was designed by Louis Schmeisser for the Rheinische Metallwaaren und Maschinenfabrik, and it was named in honor of Nikolaus von Dreyse, the famous Prussian firearms inventor. It was made from 1907 to 1915. Between 1909 and 1915 an enlarged version was made in 9mm Parabellum chambering, but these were not made in great quantity and are now in the collector category. The following remarks apply to the 7.65mm (.32 auto) version only.

On appearance alone, the Dreyse could not compete with the sleeker outlines of contemporary Walther, Mauser, and Browning designs. In spite of its strange shape, the Dreyse does have several good points. The slide serrations are located at the forward end of the gun, a placement which gives good leverage for retraction. An indicator pin protrudes at the rear of the slide when the striker is cocked. Removal of the left grip and the large sideplate beneath it exposes the entire internal mechanism for cleaning or repair. There is one interesting but operationally useless feature—a hinged barrel and slide unit. By pushing a cross-latch at the rear of the frame, the entire top assembly can be tipped upward, exposing the top of the frame. This does not, however, give access to the chamber, nor does it aid further takedown.

Flat springs are used at three points in the Dreyse. One of these is the safety positioning spring, which is of rather heavy stock, is not flexed far, and rarely breaks. The trigger bar is split and tempered to be its own spring, and here, again, breakage is infrequent. Number three is the extractor, which is long and narrow and subject to more mechanical stress than the other two. Failure of these is not unusual, but replacements are available since this is a part that has been as of late, commercially reproduced.

Aside from the relative fragility

The extractor (arrow) is perhaps the most severely flexed spring in the Dreyse Model 1907. Breakage is not uncommon; but, new replacements are available.

of the extractor, the Dreyse is really not a bad design. The grip angle is too straight, the grip frame too short for all but the smallest hands, and the frame shape sets the action too high, causing much muzzle-whip when the gun is fired. The takedown system, which involves depressing a bushing surrounding the barrel at the muzzle, is fairly difficult. In fact, if you happen to have your face over the bushing during takedown, and it gets away, it can be hazardous to your health—wear safety glasses.

In proper working order, the Dreyse is a reliable pistol, and adequate for its intended purpose as a pocket gun. Unfortunately for the Rheinmetall factory at Sommerda, there were several other pistols of its era which looked and handled better.

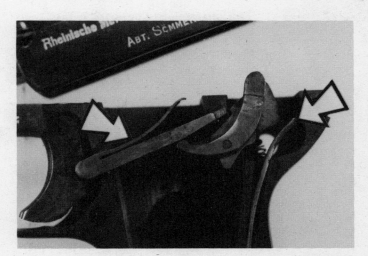

Left arrow points to the trigger bar which is split and tempered to be its own spring. Arrow on right points to the flat blade spring that positions the safety. Both of these springs are sturdy—breakage seldom takes place.

F.L. SELBSTLADER
D.R.G.M. 625263-633251

Langenhan Pistol

The Langenhan Gewehr und Fahr-radfabrik was founded in 1842 and continued in business under family management until 1945. Just after the beginning of WW I the German government commissioned the firm to produce a pistol designed by Fritz Langenhan to serve as a secondary military side arm. The initial production in 7.65mm (.32 auto) was never offered for commercial sale, being entirely a military issue. The gun was later made in 6.35mm (.25 auto) chambering, and these were sold on the commercial market. Getting back to the .32, its superficial resemblance to the Browning Model 1900 and the "FL" monogram on its grips being similar to the "FN" trademark led some to believe that the gun was merely a German imitation of the Browning, intended to mislead the unwary buyer. Since the gun was never released on the commercial market, this theory doesn't hold up.

Since the name "Langenhan" does not appear on the gun, most people know it by its markings as the "F.L. Selbstlader" (Fritz Langenhan Self-loader). During its time of production, there were several small changes made in the design, but the basic appearance remained the same.

Not very much has been written about the Langenhan, but those who have covered it have usually termed it to be dangerous because of its separate breech block and the method used to retain it. I can't entirely agree. The breech block is held in the slide by a heavy stirrup-shaped part which is pivoted on the slide to bring a bar of solid steel down into a rectangular cut, through which it also contacts an identical cut in the top of the breech block—a very strong arrangement. When the stirrup is down, it is secured in place by a large screw with milled edges which enters from the rear of the gun, and it is this arrangement which has given rise to the "dangerous" label. If this screw becomes loose and backs out to the point that it clears its aperture in the stirrup, the locking bar can lift, releasing the breech block. This occurrence would require that: (A) the screw was not adequately tightened and set in place; and (B) the shooter was so inept or dense that he failed to notice a very large screw hanging loose at the rear of his pistol. Given the circumstances above, however, it could happen. The obvious preventive measure is to check the screw whenever you plan to use the gun.

Here the pistol is shown partially disassembled. The left arrow indicates the locking screw for the stirrup-piece. The right arrow points to the stirrup, shown lifted. Be sure the locking screw is *tight*.

As in most pistols of this vintage, the Langenhan has the usual quota of blade-type springs, powering the trigger bar, positioning the safety lever, and so on. The only one that is any cause for real concern is the extractor which is tempered to be its own spring. On several examples I've seen, the extractor beak is rather thin, and several cases of breakage have been observed. Parts availability is almost nil, so any replacements would have to be made by a gunsmith.

The Langenhan is well-made of good materials, and as long as the takedown screw is kept tight, it makes a dependable shooter. Grips are of black molded hard rubber on most of these guns, are well-supported and more susceptible to age-scaling than breakage. Some early production pieces were made with grips of wood. Considering its rather brief period of manufacture, from 1915 to around 1918, the Langenhan will soon be considered more in the realm of the collector than the shooter.

O.W.A. Pistol

This Austrian O.W.A. pistol is proof-dated 1922 and has a four-digit serial number.

This interesting little .25 automatic was made for only a short time, from around 1920 to 1925..The letters in the monogram at the top of the grips stand for the name of the maker, the Osterreichische Werke Anstalt (Austrian Factory Institute). According to Dr. Mathews, in Volume I of *Firearms Identification,* there may have been some connection between this firm and O.W.G. which later became Waffenfabrik Steyr. This particular pistol, however, is not related to any Steyr design. In his closing remarks on this gun, Dr. Mathews says, "Like most of the non-Browning types of pistols, the O.W.A. is unnecessarily complicated." I have only the greatest respect for the late professor and his work, but in this case, he made a little mistake. On the contrary, the O.W.A. is outstandingly simple with fewer parts than most pistols and an easy access to those parts that is almost without parallel.

At the left rear of the barrel extension is a lever which, when turned upward, will release the barrel unit to pivot up, turning on its hinge screw at the forward end of the frame. The breech block may now be removed from the underside of the barrel unit, and the dovetailed left sideplate may be slid upward off the frame, exposing all of the internal mechanism parts. The left grip panel and the safety catch remain attached to the sideplate.

This is an internal hammer pistol with a slip-off trigger bar which requires no mechanical disconnector. The magazine release is at the lower rear of the grip frame and is pushed forward, toward the magazine, to release. The manual safety is a sliding type, located just above the top rear corner of the left grip panel. Moving it forward directly blocks the hammer. The recoil spring is positioned above the barrel, and a stud on its guide connects it to a recess in the top of the breech block.

There is only one flat spring to be concerned about, and this one powers both the sear and the magazine catch. It is not flexed severely in normal operation, and the only breakage that occurs is from metal fatigue after long use. No parts are available, but this little spring is very simple and easy to make either from flat stock or wire.

The ejector, located in the left forward wing of the breech block,

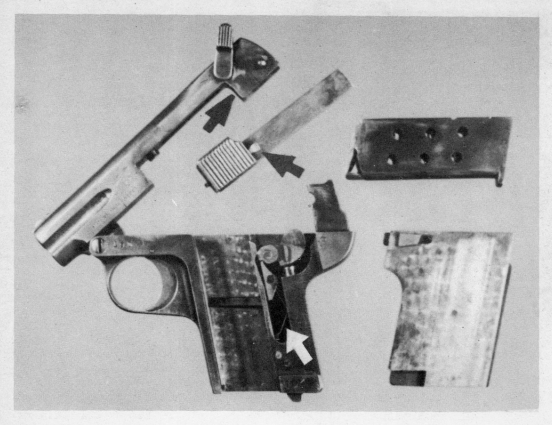

The black arrow at upper left points to the slightly peened edge of the barrel extension, caused by impact of the ejector, indicated by the other black arrow. The white arrow points to the flat sear and magazine catch spring.

is kept in retracted position by a coil spring, emerging to strike the base of the cartridge only when the rear portion of the ejector impinges on the lower rear projection of the barrel extension. The point of impact is an outside edge, and this part of the barrel unit does not seem to be as well-hardened as other parts. After long use, the edge is likely to show some peening. This can be leveled easily, but as this is an outside surface, there will be a small bright spot which will need to be touched up.

Original grips are of black molded hard rubber, a material which often becomes brittle with age. In this case, though, both grips are fully supported by the flat sides of the grip frame, so they are not often broken.

One word of caution about the internal mechanism: When the barrel and breech block are swung upward, you should avoid pulling the trigger and dropping the hammer, as this can damage the rear wall of the magazine well.

Bayard Model 1908 Pistol

A few others arrived later, but for the first few years of its production, this little Bayard was the smallest pistol made in .32 and .380 chambering. It was also produced in .25 caliber, and the manufacturer was the Anciens Etablissements Pieper factory in Herstal, Belgium.

Its top-mounted recoil spring and the ejection port just above the right grip may remind you of the 1900 Browning, but there the resemblance ends. The little Bayard is an interesting pistol, but there are some points in the design that can be detrimental to its dependability.

The extractor serves as its own blade-type spring and must be flexed rather severely during installation. More of these snap during disassembly and reassembly than in actual use. Unless it becomes absolutely necessary, the extractor should not be removed.

Blade-type springs are also used to power the sear-trip in the trigger bar, the trigger return, and the magazine catch. The last two named are tensioned by opposite ends of the same spring. The sear and hammer springs are round-wire torsion types and not as susceptible to breakage.

The springs, however, are not the most troublesome factor in this design. The disconnector system is a nightmare. There is no direct slide-activated disconnection of the trigger bar and sear. Instead, there is a slip-off tumbler mounted on the trigger bar, and a separate hammer detent, a sort of auxiliary sear, which holds the hammer at full cock until the detent is pushed down by the closing slide. This detent and the sear-trip tumbler are very small and relatively fragile parts, and their engagement is quite delicate. When all parts are crisp and new, the system works fairly well. When any of these things become a little worn, the gun often tends to fire more than one shot for each pull of the trigger.

The extractor (arrow) is long, narrow and serves as its own spring. More of these snap or break during assembly and disassembly than in actual use.

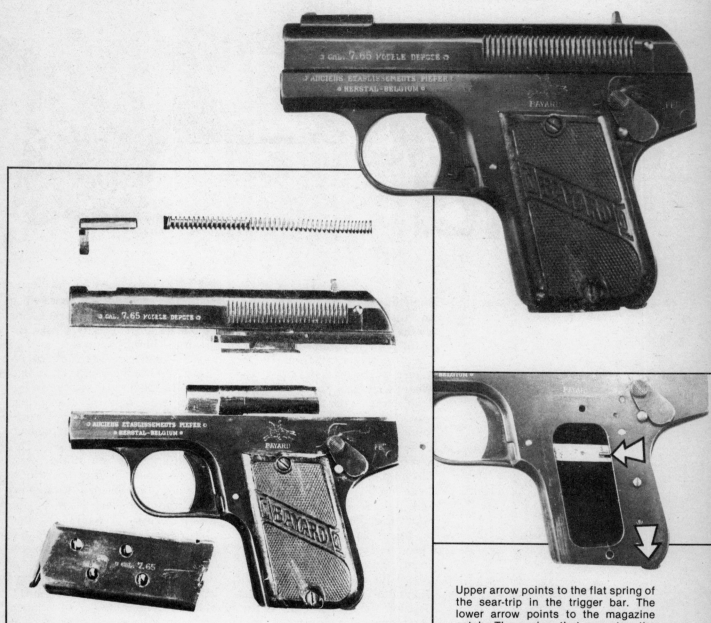

In this field-stripped view, the cylindrical portion (extending above the frame) is the recoil spring housing. The barrel is directly above the trigger, housed in the forward portion of the frame proper.

Upper arrow points to the flat spring of the sear-trip in the trigger bar. The lower arrow points to the magazine catch. The spring that operates the catch also serves as the trigger return spring—it's tensioned at both ends and therefore gets a heavy workout in normal functioning.

The Bayard is not a true hammerless—it has a pivoting internal hammer. Its manual safety is fairly positive, but is no insurance against the fragility of those tiny parts in the firing system. The only really safe way to carry it would be with the magazine full and chamber empty. In the .32, this gives you five shots. In the .380, four.

Replacement parts are definitely a problem. Try the used-parts dealers, and if they can't help, the only way is to find a gunsmith who is familiar with this gun, and have the parts made.

Lignose Einhand Pistol

Sometime between 1910 and 1913, an Austrian named Witold Chylewski designed a small pocket pistol with one unusual feature. The trigger-shaped front of the trigger guard was movable, and when pulled back to meet the trigger it retracted the slide. The pistol could thus be cocked and the first round from the magazine loaded in a one-hand operation. This was the first of the "Einhand" pistols, and Chylewski had about 100 samples made up by Societe Industrielle Suisse (later S.I.G.) for promotional purposes. In 1919 he was successful in selling the idea to Theodor Bergmann who subsequently leased production of pistols of his own design, using the "Einhand" feature, to Aktien Gesellschaft Lignose of Berlin. The Lignose Einhand pistols were produced in Lignose-owned facilities in Suhl between 1920 and 1932. In addition to two models of the Einhand, of differing handle lengths, identical guns were also made lacking the one-hand feature.

These pistols are of excellent quality in both materials and workmanship. They are not true hammerless guns, as they have a pivoting internal hammer. At the lower part of the upper frame extension, just below the slide, there is a small pin that protrudes when the internal hammer is cocked. The manual safety directly blocks the sear and limits its travel to such an extent that the slide can't be retracted if the hammer is down and the safety in on-safe position.

There are only two flat springs used in the design. One is a heavy two-pronged spring, mounted on the frame inside the right grip, which grips the end of the safety pivot to hold it in its two positions. The other flat spring is located inside the front extension of the frame, below the recoil spring, and has riveted studs which retain and position the sliding cocking piece. The safety positioning spring is heavy, and its prongs are not severly flexed, so breakage is not a hazard. The other spring is much thinner. With the pistol assembled, it can't be pushed too far, as it is stopped by the recoil spring. With the gun disassembled, however, this spring can be flexed far beyond its limits and often is during amateur efforts at complete takedown. Replacement parts are virtually unobtainable, and making one of these springs can be difficult. It is a simple, straight spring, but the proper placement of the riveted studs is a critical point.

The only other flat spring in this design is the two-pronged safety positioning spring (arrow), screw-mounted to the frame.

The cocking piece retaining stud (smaller arrow at left) and the positioning stud behind it are both riveted to a flat spring which lies in the forward frame extension. Right arrow indicates disconnector which is riveted to the trigger bar.

The disconnector is an upward projection of the trigger bar, but this part is not integral, it is attached to the bar by two rivets. It is also of fairly thin steel. There is no potential for damage in normal operation, but it would be easy to deform or break this part during complete disassembly.

The original grips are of molded hard rubber, and the left grip is unsupported at center and lower edge, a situation that often leads to breakage. No commercial replacements are available.

While the Einhand pistols are quite reliable and make good personal protection pieces, their scarcity puts them more in the realm of the collector.

Lignose Einhand, field-stripped. Note the separate cocking piece.

Schwarzlose Model 1908 Pistol

Andreas Wilhelm Schwarzlose is not usually accorded the recognition he deserves. Among war scholars he is occasionally remembered as the designer and maker of one of the first successful heavy machine guns. His contributions to automatic pistol design are often overlooked. For example: Most of us take it for granted that on most of the medium to large pistols the slide will lock open after the last shot. Andreas Schwarzlose did this first in 1898. In the same model, he was the first to use a turning-bolt locking system in a handgun, a feature echoed in the ultra-modern .44 Auto Mag pistol.

In 1908, Schwarzlose began production of a 7.65mm (.32 auto) pistol which was totally unique among pocket guns. Since most fixed-barrel pocket pistols in this caliber are said to have a "blowback" action, the proper term for this Schwarzlose system would be "blow-forward." The pistol has a solid, fixed standing breech that is integral with the frame and a movable slide/barrel unit which travels forward on firing. The sequence works this way: When the gun is fired, the friction of the bullet in the slightly tapered bore carries the slide/barrel unit forward, compressing the recoil spring. The ex-tractor, attached to the solid standing breech, grips the rim of the fired case, and as the forward moving chamber clears the case end, an ejector projection on the tail of the barrel unit kicks it out. As the unit reaches its full travel, a lower projection nudges the top cartridge in the magazine from beneath the feed lips, and the recoil spring snaps the slide/barrel unit back to scoop the round into the chamber. Firing one of these is an interesting experience, as the recoil is rather sharp because of that non-moving breech block, and the subsequent mechanical action produces a mild after-shock that somehow just feels *wrong*. This may well be one of the reasons for the pistol's lack of acceptance and its discontinuance after only three years of production.

Internally, the design has other unusual features. The hammer is

The 1908 Schwarzlose, field-stripped, right side. The sear can be seen in the rear extension of the barrel, and the extractor can be seen protruding from the standing breech.

In this left side view, the internal hammer is visible inside the receiver. Note the large chip at the top forward corner of the grip panel.

much like those in many European internal hammer revolvers with a firing pin point an integral part of the hammer body. There is a grip-type safety, but not in the usual location—it's at the front of the grip frame, below the trigger guard, and is pivoted at the lower edge of the frontstrap. A vertically moving button on the left side of the frame behind the trigger can lock the grip safety in depressed position, out of operation. The sear is located in the rear tail of the slide/barrel unit and contacts the hammer at its top, on the left side, to cock it as the action closes.

The design uses several flat springs, but the only one that is flexed severely enough for occasional breakage is the hammer spring, the lower end of which also powers the magazine catch. If this one should break, it is not a complicated part and would be simple to reproduce. Parts are, of course, totally unobtainable.

The most frequently notable casualties on the Schwarzlose are the grips, made of black hard rubber with molded checkering. These are retained by a single screw on each side at the lower edge, and I rather imagine that the sharp recoil of this little gun may be a factor in their tendency to chip and break.

Replacements must be handmade.

During the time of its manufacture, the pistol was imported and sold in the U.S. by the Warner Arms Corporation of Brooklyn, New York. When Schwarzlose discontinued the gun in 1911, the Warner Company bought the remaining parts and for a year or two assembled the pistols in New

York. Many of these will have not only the original German factory markings, but also the Warner "W.A.C." monogram on the grip panels. When the supply of Schwarzlose parts ran out, the Warner Company came up with a disaster of its own design, but that's another story. (See: The Warner "Infallible" Pistol.)

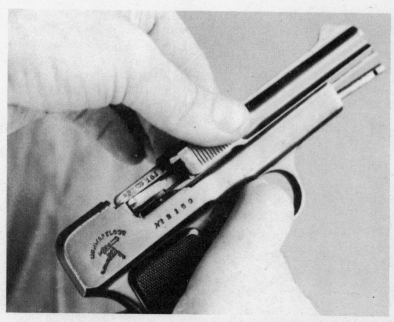

For initial loading, the slide/barrel unit of the Schwarzlose is moved forward in this manner. The rod protruding below the barrel is the recoil spring guide which is also the takedown key.

Warner Infallible Pistol

The Warner Infallible pistol shown is a later Davis-Warner type, made in Assonet, Massachusetts.

After their marketing of the Schwarzlose Model 1908 pistol proved to be somewhat less than successful, the Warner Arms Corporation of Brooklyn, New York, became interested in a design by Andrew Fyrberg of Worcester, Massachusetts, the inventor responsible for many of the features of the Iver Johnson and Harrington & Richardson revolvers. On this occasion his efforts produced a .32 automatic pistol which was manufactured by Warner beginning in 1913, the same year their factory was being moved to Norwich, Connecticut. In 1917, the Warner firm was merged with the N. R. Davis Company of Assonet, Massachusetts, and production of the gun was continued at that location until 1919, when the gun and its maker passed from the scene.

The pistol was named "The Infallible," a designation that, in retrospect, has proved somewhat amusing. It was as odd looking, in its own way, as the Schwarzlose. It has a fixed external barrel that resembles the ones on early top-break revolvers, having a thin top-rib with an integral front sight. Rather than a conventional slide, there is a round internal bolt with a large cocking knob at the rear, cross-pinned to rods above it

which extend forward to twin recoil springs. The pistol is a true hammerless, using a hollow striker with a sear detent at its lower rear edge. There are two separate safety catches. A lever type is located at the top forward corner of the left grip, and the on-safe position is toward the rear. The second one is rather weird and is a narrow leaf recessed in the upper curve of the backstrap. To operate this, you push a button on the left rear flat of the frame and use a fingernail to pull the leaf downward, releasing the button to lock it in position. This action compresses the sear spring and mechanically blocks the sear, until the same button is pressed to release it. If the pistol were hurriedly grabbed with this safety applied, you'd know it, as the rear tip of that little leaf is *sharp*.

The design is not entirely without good points. In comparison with others of its time, the magazine is very sturdy and well-made, and the magazine release is ingenious. It consists of a semicircular button recessed into the lower part of the frontstrap with twin bars extending to the rear where a crosspiece contacts a slot in the lower rear spine of the magazine.

Warner Infallible, field-stripped. The upper arrow points to the bolt retaining pin, which contacts the recoil spring rods (middle arrow), to keep the bolt in the gun. Lower arrow indicates the odd sear-block safety and its release button.

The weakest point in the design is that the bolt has no backstop whatsoever, other than the single cross-pin which connects it to the two recoil spring rods. So, when you hold this thing up in sighting position, that little cross-pin is your only insurance against wearing the bolt in your eye. When I fired one of these, this thought no doubt contributed to its lack of accuracy, as I tended to flinch.

The black molded hard-rubber grips are secured by a single screw at their rear center edge, and breakage is not unusual. As with the other parts, replacements are virtually unobtainable. I think the Infallible should be viewed as an interesting step in the evolution of the automatic pistol and left to the collectors. As a shooter, I wouldn't want to depend on it.

Sauer Model 1913 Pistol

When J. P. Sauer und Sohn of Suhl first entered the field of automatic pistols, it was in connection with the production of a pistol designed by Georg Roth of Vienna. The Roth-Sauer was short-lived, and soon after this the Sauer factory began production of a small, well-made .32 pocket automatic. It was made from 1913 to 1930, at which time it was redesigned to become the Behordenmodell ("Authority Model"). Around 1920, or shortly thereafter, a smaller version of the pistol was offered in 6.35mm.

The Model 1913 is a very compact, beautifully engineered pistol with several unusual features and very few weak points. Within the trigger guard, above the trigger, there is a flat lever which can be pushed upward to lock the slide in open position. To release it, you simply pull the trigger. Assuming the gun is in good working order, the disconnector will prevent the striker from falling, leaving the pistol cocked and ready for the first shot. The magazine catch is located in a conventional place—the lower rear of the grip frame—but it is pushed forward, toward the magazine, to release it. The trigger bar/disconnector system defies description to anyone lack-ing an engineering degree, since it operates on a rocking principle with its action controlled by precisely machined steps within the trigger. It's fortunate that it seldom breaks, as repair might be difficult for even an experienced gunsmith who was not thoroughly familiar with it.

Flat springs are used in three locations. The rear sight, which is also the latch for the slide endcap and the key to the takedown system, is tempered to be its own spring. The extractor is also in this category. When either of these breaks, the part will probably have to be made by a gunsmith, unless you can locate a replacement among the used-parts dealers. The trigger bar and magazine catch are powered by opposite ends of the same spring, which if broken, is not difficult to make.

The hollow striker seldom breaks its sear beak, but extensive dry-firing will often snap off the firing pin point. These can be re-pointed without much difficulty. Oddly enough, modern replacements for this part are available for the limited production Behordenmodell, which uses a striker of slightly larger diameter, but not for the Model 1913.

Original grips are of black

The striker spring guide is mounted solidly inside the slide endpiece. The guide seldom breaks, but if bent can jam the striker and deform the spring.

The grips are held in place by a pivoting plate which locks into recesses on each side of the magazine well. The panels are centrally unsupported, and the hard rubber will often crack (arrow).

molded hard rubber, and the centrally located screw does not contact the frame. It serves only to turn a flat plate inside the grips which locks into recesses at the front and rear of the magazine well. Broken or cracked grips are a very common occurrence, and here again, replacements are available for the Behordenmodell, but not the 1913.

If the gun is in excellent, near-new condition, a Model 1913 would be of more interest to a collector of automatic pistols than to anyone wanting a pistol for practical use.

One of the Sauer's strong points is its extractor (arrow)—it's tempered to be its own spring, is well-designed and seldom breaks.

Sauer Model 38H Pistol

(Above) This Sauer Model 38H pistol is a mid-wartime type. It still has the safety lever but lacks the Sauer markings on the slide.

With an eye on the success of the Walther double-action pistols introduced in 1929, the renowned J. P. Sauer firm of Suhl began experimenting with double-action designs as early as 1932, under the direction of Chief Design Engineer Otto Zehner. Their first efforts were in the direction of incorporating a double-action firing system into the pistol they were then producing, the Behordenmodell. Then, in late 1937, an entirely new design emerged, to be produced as the Modell 38H.

In addition to having a double-action trigger system, the 38H was unique in another way—its pivoting hammer was completely enclosed by the slide. A lever on the left side of the frame at the top forward edge of the grip panel can be pulled down to cock the inside hammer. When the hammer is cocked, pulling the lever downward will uncock the gun, letting the hammer down gently as the lever is released. The spring which returns the cocking lever is a round-wire torsion type, with its upper arm bearing on the lever and its other end powering the sear-trip piece that accomplishes the uncocking operation. The spring partially encircles the lever pivot stud on the grip frame, and when the

lever is used, the spring is rather severely flexed, its two ends nearly meeting at the bottom of the arc. This spring occasionally breaks, but more often it simply becomes weak, with insufficient tension to fully return the cocking lever. Replacement of this little spring is not a job for the amateur, but any competent gunsmith can easily make one, cold-formed from round-wire stock.

The long trigger bar, which lies in a shallow well on the right side of the pistol, has a rear tip that is both intricately shaped and rather delicate. When this tip breaks off, you are presented with a great problem. This part has not been commercially duplicated, and making one is a gunsmith's nightmare. I've done it *once*. Don't ask. Your only hope is to try the used-parts dealers, and these things are in short supply. Fortunately, they don't often break.

The hammer of the 38H is designed to rebound after it strikes the firing pin, the rebound controlled by crescent-shaped cuts in the top of the hammer strut. As made, the system works perfectly. If, however, the hammer strut becomes even slightly bent, either forward or to the rear, the rebound will cease to function. This can

The arrow points to the trigger bar. This one is intact—they seldom break.

When the cocking lever is operated, the cocking lever spring (arrow) is severely flexed.

cause the hammer to jam at full cock, or fail to engage the double-action trigger bar when down. The hammer strut will rarely be deformed during normal use of the gun. Most damage occurs from improper assembly or disassembly.

The Model 38H has a magazine safety which operates to block the trigger bar when the magazine is out of the gun, a precaution against someone forgetting that there is a live round in the chamber when unloading. This small spring-powered lever, mounted on the frame beneath the right grip, is operated by a stud on the right side of the magazine. The engagement is fairly delicate. A loose magazine, or even one not original to the pistol, can fail to release the magazine safety, locking the trigger. In this case, no need to fix it—just remove the little abomination. There is no excuse for not knowing that the chamber is loaded, as this pistol is equipped with a very obvious pin-type indicator, which protrudes from the upper rear of the slide when a round is in the chamber.

The Sauer Model 38H has a strong and well-designed extractor and ejector and a very good safety which rolls a solid bar of steel around to block the hammer. Even

though it was regularly produced only in the .32 chambering, and not the supposedly magic .380, both shooters and collectors compete for every one that turns up for sale.

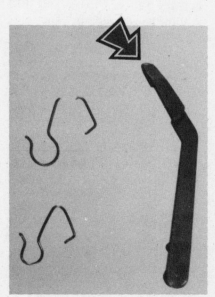

The arrow points to the broken end of the trigger bar. To the left, a broken original cocking lever spring, and a replacement made of round wire.

Sauer WTM 1924 Pistol

(Above) Sauer WTM 1924 pistol, left side. Grips are replacements of ivory, retained by tiny screws.

Observing the success of Walther's tiny Model 9 pistol, the renowned J. P. Sauer firm of Suhl began producing their Westen-Taschen Modell (Vest-Pocket Model) in 1924. Almost as small as the Walther, the Sauer WTM is only 10.5 centimeters in length. The little gun was made for the 6.35mm (.25 auto) cartridge and is easily recognizable by the serrations both at the rear and near the front of the slide on each side. This pistol was produced for only four years, and was redesigned to become the WTM 1928.

The WTM 1924, like many of the early European pistols, is made like a fine watch with much hand-fitting of small and intricate parts. In spite of this, it is quite reliable, and breakage is rare. The breech block is a separate unit within the slide and is held in place at the rear by a lever-like catch which extends from the back of the breech block.

The arrow points to the beak of the breech block latch. Wear or breakage here can allow the breech block to slip forward in the slide.

This catch is powered by a V-type narrow spring which lies in a shallow recess in the side of the breech block, and this spring is the only one in the gun which breaks with any frequency.

When the breech block is removed during disassembly, this spring is also subject to loss. One end of it enters a hole in the end of the catch lever, and this tends to hold it in place. If the catch lever is moved, however, it will easily detach from the breech block, and the spring can flick away. There is absolutely no parts source for the WTM 1924, so any replacement would have to be made by a gunsmith. This applies to any of the other parts as well.

This is a true hammerless, striker-fired pistol, and the striker is a conventional hollow type, with breakage no more frequent than in others of this design. At the rear of its spring, there is a combination guide and indicator, the rear tip of which protrudes when the gun is cocked. Again, during disassembly, this little guide/indicator can easily be lost.

The flat external portion of the manual safety lever is tempered to be its own positioning spring. Since it is not flexed to any degree in normal use, it rarely breaks.

Sauer's intricate trigger bar and disconnector assembly (arrow) rarely will malfunction, but when it does, it's difficult to repair.

The arrow points to the manual safety lever which is its own positioning spring. This rarely breaks except during improper disassembly.

Those I've seen broken were all victims of amateur disassembly.

The trigger bar/disconnector system of this gun is beautifully engineered, but its intricacy and small size make it difficult to repair in the rare cases when its tiny internal spring breaks. Fortunately, this doesn't happen often.

The original black molded hard-rubber grips of the WTM 1924, with their unique screwless retention system, are well-supported, but can become brittle with age. When they chip or break, it is usually necessary to employ another means of keeping the hand-made replacements on the gun. The gun shown in the photos has had this alteration, as its genuine ivory grips are retained by a tiny screw.

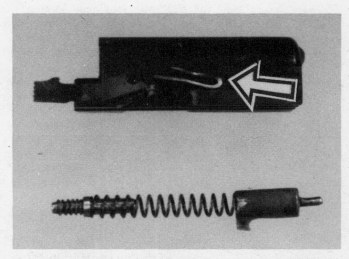

Arrow indicates the small V-type spring which powers the breech block latch. Below, the striker, spring, and guide/indicator, the latter easily lost during disassembly.

Mauser HSc Pistol

In 1934, the great Mauser Werke slightly redesigned their 1910/14 pocket pistols, the main change being a more comfortable grip shape. Even so, they were still losing a lot of sales to the Walther PP and PPK, which offered double-action on the first shot. Shortly thereafter, the Mauser Modell HSc emerged, and in some ways, it was superior to the Walthers. Incidentally, for those who have always wondered, the "HS" stands for "Hahn Selbstspannung"—Hammer, Self-cocking. The small "c" designates it as the third model, accepted for regular production. It was preceded by the HSa and HSb models, which were experimental only.

The Mauser HSc is one of the very few pistols which can claim a safety system that is absolutely positive. When the safety lever is rotated downward, the rear portion of the firing pin is moved up into the top of the slide, completely out of the reach of the hammer. To further guard against inertial firing if the pistol is dropped, there is a cylindrical projection on top of the firing pin which fits into a corresponding well in the slide, completely immobilizing the pin when the safety is on. A manual safety is not really very necessary on a double-action pistol, but this one is of particular value when loading. After the first round has been run into the chamber, the safety may be pushed down and the trigger pulled. The hammer will strike only the rear of the breech block, and there is not the slightest possibility of accidental firing—assuming, of course, that no one has tampered with the mechanism or installed homemade parts. Also, since the safety does not hold the trigger to the rear, as in the Walthers, the safety lever may be left in the "safe" position after loading, if you wish.

The HSc does have one or two points which occasionally cause trouble. The firing pin point has a very slim forward section, with a slight enlargement or "collar" near its tip. This arrangement is necessary because of the minimum clearances encountered during assembly and disassembly. The largest number of these pistols were of wartime manufacture, and the heat treatment of firing pins was often not up to the usual fine Mauser standards of control. As a result, the firing pin tip is often somewhat fragile. Fortunately, newly-made replacements have recently become available.

The HSc is equipped with an in-

Arrow points to the operating surface of the slide hold-open device which is susceptible to wear and breakage. Check excessive wear or burring.

genious slide hold-open device which also doubles as a magazine safety, blocking the trigger bar when the magazine is not in the pistol. Unlike other guns which have a last shot hold-open device, the Mauser has an automatic release. With the slide open, the insertion of a magazine, loaded or empty, will trip the hold-open latch and allow the slide to run forward. The hold-open device is made of stamped sheet steel, and here again, the heat treatment was sometimes done with less than the usual care. The rear tip can be too soft and will either show excessive wear or burring. When this happens, the gun will still function, but after the last shot, the slide will stay open as caught by the magazine follower, not the hold-open, and the slide will snap closed as soon as the magazine is pulled out. It is possible to add a spot of steel weld to a worn or burred hold-open, recut it to shape, and give it the proper heat treatment.

The original grips on almost all HSc pistols were made of walnut and were relatively thin. At the top front corner on each side a sharply-tapered projection extends forward, and since the grain in the grip panels is more or less vertical, this small tip often breaks off.

Currently-made replacements are available, but these are plastic and lack the feel and good appearance of the originals.

The only other ailment of the HSc is what might be called "sleepy trigger spring syndrome." The rear terminus of the trigger spring also supplies upward tension to the trigger bar, and after long years of use, this round-wire, torsion-type spring can lose some of its power. Cold reshaping of both ends of the spring is often possible and will usually cure the problem. Also, replacements are available at very low cost.

Several years after WW II, the Mauser Werke resumed the manufacture of the HSc, but the new version is a slight redesign, and not all of the parts will interchange. All of the remarks above refer to the pre-war and wartime pistol.

While the Mauser HSc is a good pistol, most of those produced were made during WW II. The heat treatment of the wartime firing pins was often not up to Mauser standards—many break, but new pins *are* available.

Mauser Model 1934 pistol in 7.65mm.

Mauser Model 1910/34 Pistol

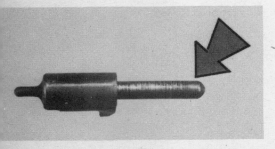

The spring guide (arrow) on this Mauser is an integral part of the striker; however, it will occasionally break away from the striker body.

Most gun people simply refer to the older Mauser Pocket Pistols as the "Model 1910." To keep the nomenclature correct, here's a brief outline: The first of this model, the true Model 1910, was made in 6.35mm (.25 auto) only. Beginning in 1914, the gun was also offered in 7.65mm (.32 auto), so the early .32 is properly called Model 1914. Then, in 1934, the pistol was slightly reworked in both calibers, creating the Model 1934, the main change being a more comfortable grip shape.

The basic pistol was designed in an era of complicated, beautifully fitted internal mechanisms, and when everything is working properly, its functioning is flawless. As with most of the early designs, however, flat springs were used at several critical points. The trigger and safety/sear springs are this type, and the extractor, safety release button, takedown button and magazine catch all have tempered shanks, making each of these its own spring. The hold-open device is also powered by a blade spring, an extension of the magazine catch.

Of those mentioned, the one that most often fails is the safety/sear spring. Its upper arm, the one which powers the sear, flexes very little. The lower arm, which returns the safety to the "off" position when the release button is pressed, receives quite a lot of compression, and for this reason the spring frequently snaps. Fortunately, it is a lot easier to make one of these than the part-and-spring combinations. When one of these breaks, you are in real trouble. They are not among the parts that have been reproduced in recent times, and making such things as an extractor or takedown latch can be an expensive operation. Used parts for these pistols are becoming increasingly scarce.

This Mauser is a true hammerless, a striker-fired pistol, which simply means that it has a hollow combined striker/firing pin unit which travels in a round tunnel in the slide. The striker, a masterpiece of fine German machine work, has a long spring guide protruding from its hollow body, giving good support to the coil striker spring. When the pistol is cocked, the tip of this guide protrudes from the rear of the gun, indicating that the pistol is ready to fire. Occasionally, the guide will break away from the striker body and can jam the slide and deform the striker spring. Fortunately, this is one of the parts that has been recently

Chambered for the 6.35 (.25 ACP) only, the Mauser Model 1910 is slightly smaller, overall, than the Model 1934.

reproduced, as it is almost impossible to rejoin a broken guide to the striker.

The Mauser does have one quirk which might be termed a chronic ailment, but it's a thing that appears only after many years of hard usage. The rear projection of the ejector is a hold-open device for the slide, and it is powered by a very strong blade spring, an upper extension of the magazine catch. When the magazine is pushed into the gun, a small rear portion of its right feed lip will contact the ejector, pushing it into horizontal position against heavy spring tension. If the slide is open when a magazine is inserted, it will be released to run forward. Whether the slide is open or closed, the feed lip still encounters the ejector. If the magazine is slammed into the pistol, rather than being pushed gently into place, the repeated impact can eventually deform the rear part of the right feed lip. If this damage becomes severe, several things can happen. The dent in the feed lip may cause the magazine to misfeed, the open slide may not be released, or the ejector/hold-open unit, which is also a magazine safety, may fail to release its sear-blocking function, and the pistol will not fire. In this case, a new

magazine will be necessary, and remember to insert it gently.

The Mauser 1910, 1914, and 1934 pistols are finely made guns of the old European school. In practical use they are handicapped by the lack of an external hammer and double-action firing system. These points may not be important, as they are now becoming more valuable as collector guns than as shooters.

(Below) The extractor (arrow) on both the 1910 and 1934 Model Mausers is tempered to be its own spring.

(Below) Arrows indicate the location of blade-type springs: (1) extractor, (2) takedown latch, (3) trigger, (4) sear/safety, (5) safety release and (6) magazine catch.

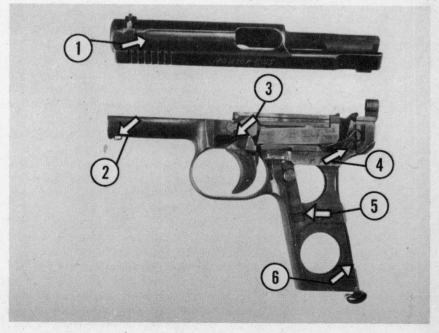

Mauser Model 1896 Pistol

The Mauser Model 1896 pistol shown above is actually the 1899 Transition Type with large-ring hammer and other differences.

I must confess that I am as susceptible to the "Mauser Mystique" as anyone. Just thinking of the "Broomhandle" brings many images to mind—"Spectre" assassin Red Grant in Ian Fleming's *From Russia With Love,* saving the life of James Bond at the gypsy camp —the hero of Gavin Lyall's *Midnight Plus One,* with a Schnellfeuer Model—but most of all, in the real world, at the Battle of Omdurman in the Sudan, on the second of September, 1898, where a young subaltern of the 21st Lancers, his saber arm stiff from an old wound, used a Model 1896 Mauser to shoot his way out of "a bit of a bad spot." It's fortunate that he had the Mauser or the world might have lost Winston Churchill that day in Africa.

The pistol was designed at Waffenfabrik Mauser in the city of Oberndorf, Germany, by Paul Mauser, Fidel Feederle and other members of the Mauser engineering department. The first prototype was completed and tested on March 15, 1895, and the gun was patented in Germany on December 11 of the same year. The pistol went into full production in 1896 and continued until 1937 with many variations to delight collectors along the way. With its long barrel and forward-positioned magazine, the pistol is at its best when the combination holster/shoulder stock is attached, making it into a light, efficient carbine. Early in the production, a relatively small number of guns chambered a special 9mm Long cartridge designed by Mauser, and in 1916 the gun was also offered in 9mm Parabellum (Luger) chambering (this is the one with the large red "9" on the grips). Primarily, though, the gun was made for the 7.63mm Mauser cartridge, known in the U.S. as the .30 Mauser. Unfortunately, this round was discontinued by the major ammunition companies a few years ago, and the supply of military surplus ammo is running very thin. When this is gone, shooters must turn to the custom loaders.

Internally, the Mauser is an engineering masterpiece, a tribute to the meticulous hand-fitting of yesteryear. It is full of neat little things such as a hammer pivot with tempered extensions on the right side which become the sear/disconnector and takedown latch springs. One can appreciate these finely polished parts—until one of them breaks. Used parts are occasionally available, but if they can't be found, the cost of making re-

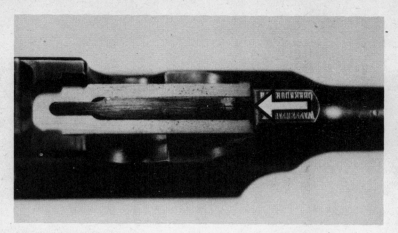

The arrow indicates the extractor, the most frequently broken part. The one shown is the older type, later shortened and with added retainer wings.

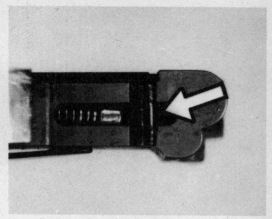

A bottom view of the sub-frame, dismounted from the pistol. The arrow at its forward end points to the rocker coupling, this one properly installed. Inverted, it will make disassembly extremely difficult. Without special tools, impossible.

placement parts for the Mauser will be relatively high.

The extractor is tempered to be its own spring and is the one part most frequently broken. Early extractors are long, narrow and straight, while later ones are shorter, wider and have retaining wings on each side at the front. Both types are flange-stepped into the bolt at the rear and require that the front be lifted to clear the locking projections during installation. More extractors are broken in disassembly and reassembly than in actual firing.

The tension for the adjustable rear sight is supplied by a blade-type spring, but this one is easy to reproduce. Opposite ends of one flat spring power the trigger and the magazine floorplate latch, and this one would be a bit more difficult to reproduce. The magazine uses a multiple-fold flat spring, but this could be replaced with formed round wire if necessary. The safety lever, whether an old or new type, has a tempered extension which snaps into two notches in the sub-frame for positioning, and if this should break (it rarely does), you have real trouble.

In designing the Model 1896, the Mauser people failed to allow for one thing—human error. The rocker coupling, a small crescent-shaped part with an integral pivot at its rear edge, can be installed upside down. When this is done, there is no problem in putting the gun back together. The problem surfaces when the gun fails to work properly, and you try to take it apart. One lobe of the rocker coupling will have locked firmly in front of the trigger and its spring, and no amount of force will get it past. I have seen Mauser pistols actually bent and otherwise damaged by attempts to drive a jammed action off to the rear. In the past, the usual method of correcting this situation was to drill a hole near the trigger, insert a tool to lift the coupling, and afterwards weld the hole closed and try to restore the area to original appearance. A couple of years ago, I developed a system of tools for both the early and late models which can be inserted from above to lift the rocker coupling without marring the pistol. The shape of these tools defies description, and their use is somewhat comparable to the jeweler's stroke when he cuts a diamond. I don't intend to make it sound mysterious—it just can't be explained in this limited space.

Some shooters have expressed worry about the single separate

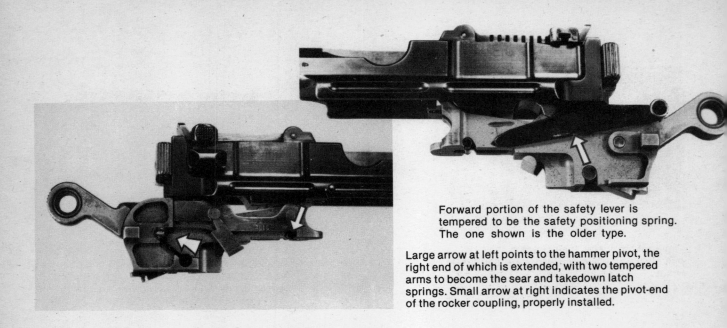

Forward portion of the safety lever is tempered to be the safety positioning spring. The one shown is the older type.

Large arrow at left points to the hammer pivot, the right end of which is extended, with two tempered arms to become the sear and takedown latch springs. Small arrow at right indicates the pivot-end of the rocker coupling, properly installed.

block of steel which retains the bolt in the Mauser, but I've never heard of an authenticated case of breakage. This durability is partially due to the efficiency of the pistol's double lug locking system, which keeps the bolt firmly locked to the barrel until the high pressure has dropped. It should also be remembered that the Mauser was always made of the very best materials, and the heat treatment of the parts was by experts.

A very few Mauser pistols originally had grips of molded hard rubber, but the great majority had wooden grip panels, and breakage has never been a problem. For those who like to shoot the "Broomhandle," the most disturbing thing today is the drastic increase in collector interest which has actually made most of them too valuable to shoot.

Franz Stock Pistols

Aside from their good design and high quality of materials and workmanship, these German automatics have one distinction—they were made in Berlin, not at Suhl which was the main center of arms production. They were made primarily in 6.35mm and 7.65mm (.25 and .32 auto) and were produced between 1922 and 1929. A very few were made in .22 chambering, but these are rare and not likely to be seen outside of collections.

There are several good points in the design of the Stock pistols, and the .25 and .32 versions are almost identical except for size. The gun contains helical coil round-wire springs only, no flat springs at all. All parts are heavy and strong with no delicate or thin systems which might be prone to breakage. The breech block is a separate removable part, retained in the slide by a hook that is integral with the rear tail of the extractor. At first glance, the striker (firing pin) appears to be like the one used in the Mauser 1910 pistol with an integral spring guide. This one, though, is not hollow. It is a solid part and not susceptible to separation of the guide extension. In case of a broken point, it could easily be re-pointed. There is a large screw at the rear of the breech block, and removal of this gives access to the striker and spring without further takedown.

Speaking of takedown, the breech block hook at the rear of the extractor is not liable to breakage in normal use, but could be broken if some ham-handed type attempted to force the breech block forward without first lifting the extractor. The manual safety lever directly blocks the sear, and there is also a magazine safety acting on the sear which prevents firing when the magazine is out.

The only real criticism I can direct at these fine pistols is in regard to the molded hard-rubber grips which are retained at top forward and lower rear corners by two screws on each side. The left grip is centrally unsupported, especially at its lower edge, and on both grips the screws are located fairly near the edges. I have seen several examples of broken and chipped grips, and no commercial replacements are available. In the unlikely event that a major part breaks, repairs will probably have to be made by a gunsmith, as the used-parts dealers seldom have parts for the Stock pistols. Still, it wouldn't hurt to try to find the parts, as you might get lucky, and a used original is always preferable to a repaired piece.

These pistols are beautiful pre-war examples of the German gun-making art and are of interest to both collectors and shooters.

Upper arrow points to the magazine safety. Lower arrow indicates the open side of the frame which contributes to grip breakage.

The separate breech block, showing the retaining hook (arrow) which is a part of the extractor.

French Model 1935-A Pistol

The French Model 1935-A pistol was manufactured by the Societe Alsacienne de Constructions Mecaniques (S.A.C.M.) at Cholet, France. The one shown was made during the Nazi Occupation.

On March 3, 1934 Charles Gabriel Petter patented a pistol design that was to be produced in several forms in two countries. One version of it is still in production today—the Swiss S.I.G. Neuhausen P-210. Petter's original design was adopted as military standard by France in 1935 and was designated the Modele 1935-A. The pistol was chambered for a special 7.65mm Long cartridge, like an ordinary .32 auto with a longer case and a more pointed bullet of heavier weight. The French were apparently impressed by the cartridge used in the U.S. Pedersen Device of WW I, as their 7.65mm Long is practically identical to it, and the two rounds will actually interchange.

In his design, Petter borrowed freely from existing guns but added a few excellent ideas of his own. The slide and recoil spring arrangement are Browning-style, as is the barrel locking system, although Petter used twin barrel links and a captive recoil spring. His separate sub-frame, containing the ejector, hammer, sear and springs, may have been copied after the Russian Tokarev which had first appeared in 1930. The arrangement of parts in the sub-frame, though, is an improvement

on the Tokarev system. The shape of the grip frame is particularly outstanding and is one of the most comfortable ever made. It is reminiscent of the grip shape of the Model 51 Remington pistol—another excellent design.

Petter designed a good hammer-block safety, a solid bar of steel which presents a flat surface to the hammer in firing position and rolls a convex surface around when on safe to block the hammer from the firing pin. As an added advantage, the pistol can be dry-fired with the safety applied with no danger of breaking the firing pin. If all of the parts are original, the system works perfectly. If, however, someone has replaced the firing pin with one of extra length, the gun could be fired with the safety on, as the lever blocks only the hammer face and has no effect on the trigger or sear. Before using one of these guns to any extent, the firing pin should be checked to insure that it is of original length.

There is only one blade-type spring in the 1935-A pistol. Inside the right grip panel there is a flat spring screw-mounted on the outside of the frame with a projection that enters an opening in the frame to depress the trigger bar when the magazine is withdrawn. These will

The hammer-block safety is shown turned up into the on-safe position. As long as the firing pin is of original length, the system is virtually infallible.

occasionally break, but this part is not essential to the normal operation of the pistol. If replacement is desired for collector restoration purposes, several of the used-parts dealers can supply it. If they are out of it, the part is not difficult to reproduce.

For owners of this pistol, the only real problem is the ammunition. The 7.65mm Long was never produced in any great quantity commercially, and the stock of surplus ammo in the U.S. is rapidly dwindling. Even when it can be found, many of these rounds are the old steel-cased French Military ammunition, and dead primers are very common. Original cases are very difficult to reload and require a Berdan primer. If the gun is not in fine collector condition, the Model 1935-A can be converted to function with ordinary .32 auto cartridges, and with its efficient locking system, some very warm handloads can be used.

French Model 1935-A, field-stripped. Note the sub-frame at the right, containing the hammer, hammer and sear spring, sear and ejector.

French Model 1935-S Pistol

The French Model 1935-S pistol shown was made by Manufacture d'Armes de Chatellerault (M.A.C.).

In 1939, four years after the adoption of the Petter-designed Model 1935-A, engineers at the Government Arsenal, Manufacture d'Armes de St. Etienne, produced a drastic revision of the original pistol, and it was designated the Modele 1935-S. The only features that were retained from the first design were the general style of the safety system and the package-type sub-frame firing system—both of which were considerably changed. The main idea in the redesign was to make a pistol that was easier to manufacture, allowing the production of a larger quantity in less time. Among the simplifications was the elimination of the twin locking lugs on top of the barrel, the 1935-S having a single locking shoulder which locks against the forward edge of the ejection port.

Some of the alterations were not entirely for the better. Although the general idea of the Petter hammer-block safety was used, the angle was changed, and its positive efficiency was not the same. In several of these pistols I have examined, repeated hammer impact with the safety in the on-safe position could cause the lever to flip back down to firing position—a markedly unhealthy quirk.

The beautifully contoured grip shape of the 1935-A is gone, replaced in the 1935-S by a straight, square-edged and slab-sided grip that is adequate but nothing more. The damnable magazine safety was retained, but was moved to the left side of the gun and changed to a pivoting type with a round-wire spring which is less susceptible to breakage.

As on the 1935-A, there is a cartridge indicator in the top of the slide that rises when the chamber is loaded. The 1935-S indicator is

A rear view showing the safety in off-safe position, exposing the firing pin head to the hammer face.

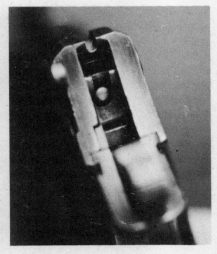

Same view showing the safety in on-safe position. Note the shielding surfaces which block the hammer face from the firing pin.

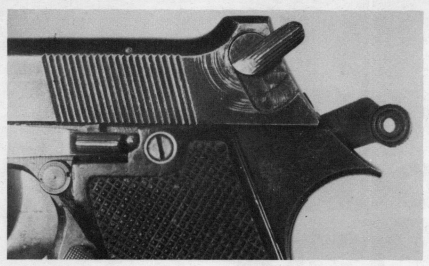

The safety lever is shown in the on-safe position. The circular marks outside the safety recess were made by careless disassembly and reassembly.

longer and powered by the safety positioning spring rather than having its own. The leverage is different, and this one is less tolerant of cartridges dropped directly into the chamber. It works best when the cartridges are fed from the magazine thus rising beneath the indicator to insure proper tripping. There is occasional breakage. This is a simple part to make, but parts are usually available from the surplus dealers.

Like the 1935-A, this pistol also uses the 7.65mm Long cartridge, and the remarks made in the section on the 1935-A pistol also apply here. The grips on both pistols are of black hard rubber with molded checkering, and they seem to be fairly tough. I've seen very few cf them broken or chipped.

This pistol was made at several arsenals and factories, and will be found with various markings: Manufacture d'Armes de St. Etienne (M.A.S.); Manufacture d'Armes de Tuile (M.A.T.); Manufacture d'Armes de Chatellerault (M.A.C.); and Societe d'Applications Generales Electriques et Mecaniques (S.A.G.E.M.). A few have been seen with the S.A.C.M. marking, indicating that the 1935-S pistol may have superseded the original model at that facility.

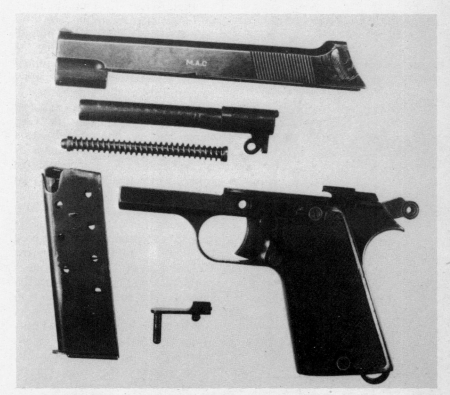

French Model 1935-S, field-stripped. In this view, the rear sub-frame is still in place.

Unique Model 52 Pistol

In these days of aluminum alloy and sheet-steel stampings, the solid feel of this French .22 automatic pleases the traditionalists. Made entirely of steel with machined parts, it's relatively heavy for its size, and its weight aids accuracy. It was marketed in the U.S. a few years ago, both under its own name and as one of the Sears models. The pistol is well-made of quality materials, but there are two quirks which tend to detract from an otherwise good design.

The most serious fault involves the firing pin retainer, a sliding plate of the same general type used on our .45 1911 pistol. On the Unique Model 52, the retainer is quite thick and heavy, and a rather large recess is cut out of the slide to accept it. At the top, on each side, this leaves a slide thickness of only $\frac{1}{32}$-inch. When the slide recoils during the firing cycle, it is the lower edge of the firing pin retainer which supplies the final pressure to cock the hammer. As this happens, a reverse pressure is transmitted to the retainer and from the retainer to the top of the slide. As a result, the thin sections on each side will often crack. I've never seen a case of actual breakage—just hairline cracks, and that's as far as it goes. It looks un-sightly, but doesn't seem to be dangerous.

Let's approach the problem from two directions—repair and prevention. Repair is fairly simple. Any competent gunsmith can close the cracks with steel weld, recut the slide surface to shape, and refinish the slide. The prevention process can be a bit more complicated. One way is to enlarge the opening in the retainer to the diameter of the firing pin body and weld the retainer to the slide at its lower edge. Then, mill a recess in the body of the firing pin and drill and tap the underside of the breech block for a small headless screw to bear on the recess and retain the firing pin. This alteration will require the services of a good gunsmith, but it will keep the trouble from happening.

There is another design feature of the Model 52 which causes no operational difficulty, but which bothers shooters who like to carry external hammer pistols with the chamber loaded. The firing pin is not an inertia type, and when the hammer is down, the firing pin point is against the rim of a chambered cartridge. In this situation, a blow on the hammer or dropping the gun on its muzzle would be likely to cause accidental firing.

Also, the Model 52 has no "safety" or "half-cock" step on the hammer, its two positions being fully cocked and down. There is a manual safety, but it blocks the trigger and has no effect on the hammer at all.

Since this pistol has a fairly heavy hammer and a strong hammer spring, this problem can be solved by converting the gun to an inertia firing pin. All that is necessary is to remove a small amount of steel from the head of the firing pin—the rear end, not the point—until the pin is exactly the same length as its tunnel in the slide. Be very careful not to shorten it too much, and don't alter the forward end in any way.

The Unique pistol was made by Fabrique d'Armes de Pyrenees in Hendaye, France, and the company is still in business. The Model 52 is no longer being made, and I have no data on the availability of parts. The only Unique pistol currently offered for sale in the U.S. is the Modele D.E.S., an Olympic-grade target gun. It is imported by Connecticut Valley Arms. CVA will definitely have *no* parts for the Model 52, but since they are in contact with the factory in France, perhaps they might be able to help.

The Unique 52's most serious fault lies in the firing pin retainer, a sliding plate of large dimensions which leaves a slide thickness of $\frac{1}{32}$-inch (arrow) in the corners of the retainer recess area.

During the final cocking stages, the firing pin retaining plate is forced upwards against the slide at its weakest point—hairline cracks (arrow) can develop.

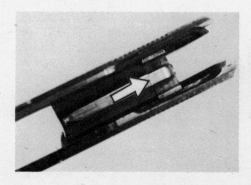

To correct the hairline cracking problem, other means can be devised to retain the firing pin, and the original retainer could be welded in place where it meets the breech block (arrow).

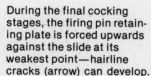

53

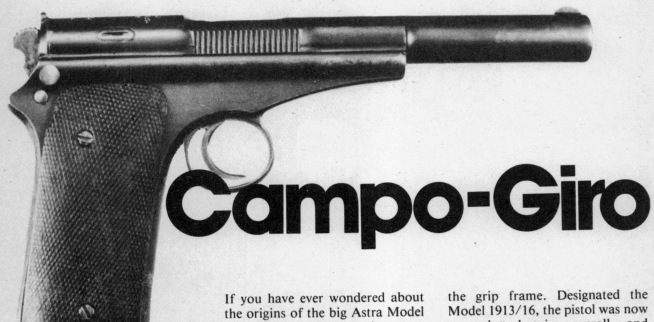

Campo-Giro

(Above and facing page) Left-, and right-side views of the Campo-Giro Model 1913/16 pistol—this example has checkered wooden grips.

If you have ever wondered about the origins of the big Astra Model 400 pistol, put this name into your mental file: Don Venancio Lopez de Caballos y Aquirre. Or, to give his title as a Spanish nobleman, the Count of Campo-Giro. In 1904, this Army officer and design engineer completed the prototype of a pistol that was finally adopted in 1913 as the standard side arm of the Spanish Military Forces. Having no manufacturing facilities, the Count arranged for the pistol to be made by a young firm which would later evolve into one of the best-known manufacturers. At that time, they were known simply as Esperanza y Unceta.

The pistols were chambered for the 9mm Bergmann-Bayard round, which in Spain came to be called the 9mm Largo. The original Model 1913 was a bit light for this round, and a recoil buffer was soon added to cushion the slide impact. On this early model, the magazine release was a pedal-like lever just behind the suspended trigger guard, and on this heavy-caliber, blow-back pistol it probably gouged a few fingers before it was changed. Three years later, when the pistol was slightly redesigned, the magazine release was moved to the right lower edge of

the grip frame. Designated the Model 1913/16, the pistol was now somewhat heavier overall, and there were other minor mechanical changes.

There are only three flat springs in the design of the Campo-Giro. The hammer spring is a heavy blade-type, but it seldom breaks. A flat spring also powers the sear, and if one of these succumbs to metal fatigue, it would be simple to reproduce. The third leaf spring is the extractor, tempered to power itself. This, also, is a relatively heavy part, and extreme flexing is not required for disassembly or reassembly, so breakage is not common. If an extractor should break, one would have to be made by a gunsmith, as there are *no* parts.

The pedal-like magazine release of the Model 1913/16, now at the bottom edge of the left grip, has a fairly thin neck and is susceptible to bending and breakage. The slide lock, an internal part which holds the slide open when the last round is fired, has twin tempered arms that act as its return springs, so perhaps these should be counted among the blade-types. This entire part is much too delicate for its purpose and must have caused difficulty during the pistol's time as a military side arm. This part is the

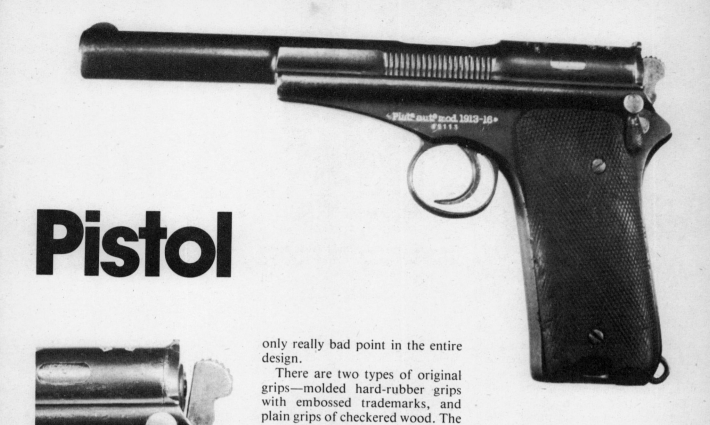

Pistol

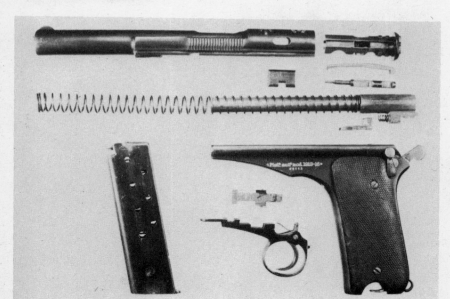

only really bad point in the entire design.

There are two types of original grips—molded hard-rubber grips with embossed trademarks, and plain grips of checkered wood. The hard-rubber type are prone to chipping and breakage, and there

Unlike the 1913 Model, the 1913/16 has a safety lever which will work only with the hammer down, lifting it slightly away from the firing pin head.

Note the extremely long and powerful recoil spring and the large number of parts. Routine disassembly, even this far, is not recommended.

In addition to the long and heavy recoil spring, the pistol has a separate buffer with a heavy spring just below the barrel to cushion the slide impact.

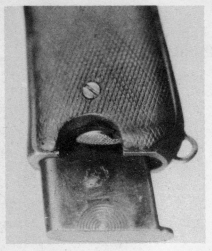

The pedal-type magazine release of the 1913/16 Model has a narrow neck and is susceptible to damage.

are no replacements, of course. Routine takedown of the Campo-Giro is not recommended, not even for those familiar with automatic pistols. Once, in a magazine article, I detailed the takedown procedure, and it covered a full page-and-a-half. The pistol is complicated, and there are several little "tricks" that are almost impossible to describe.

On November 25, 1914, Esperanza and Unceta registered the "Astra" as their trademark. Production of the Campo-Giro ceased in 1921, and in the same year, the Astra Model 400 appeared and was adopted by the Spanish Military. Its relation to the Campo-Giro is obvious.

The separate breech block is turned on its side in this position for disassembly and reassembly. Note the long spring-steel extractor, which will lie on top when the breech block is back in place.

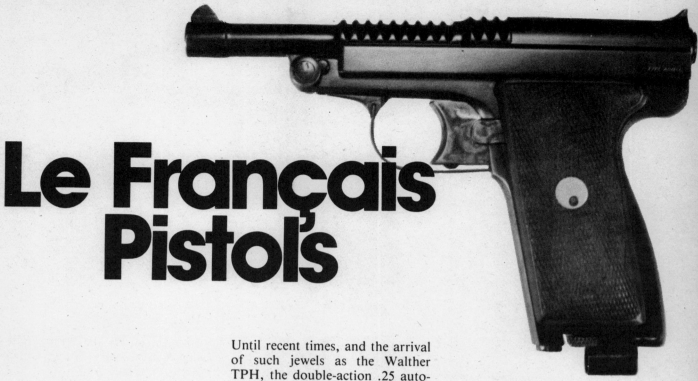

Le Français Pistols

This Le Français, Model 1928, is chambered for the 9mm Browning Long cartridge.

Until recent times, and the arrival of such jewels as the Walther TPH, the double-action .25 automatic was not seen in any quantity. There were only four in existence: The Walther PP and PPK (experimental in .25 caliber, very rare); the Austrian Wiener "Little Tom" (the first true double-action pocket pistol); the Czech Model 45; and the Le Français.

This excellent little French pistol, which owes nothing to Browning design except its cartridge, was made by the Manufacture Francaise d'Armes et Cycles de St. Etienne, usually abbreviated as Manufrance. The guns were made in two basic types: The Modele de Poche (Pocket Model), with a very short barrel and low profile striker housing; and the "Type Policeman" (Police Model) with a longer barrel and domed striker housing. The design emerged in 1914, based on a pattern by Monsieur Mimard, founder of the firm, and was developed by the Manufrance Research Department.

It's an excellent design. The firing system is double-action *only,* each shot requiring a complete travel of the sliding trigger which pushes the inclined sear to both cock and release the internal striker. Thus, the pistol is never cocked

except at the instant of firing. There is no manual safety and no need for one. The helical coil recoil spring is housed vertically in the front part of the grip frame, and flat steel arms on each side, beneath the grips, connect it to the slide. Operating a lever on the right side of the frame releases the barrel, allowing it to tip upward for loading the last round directly into the chamber—no need to draw back the slide. In fact, many Le Francais pistols have no slide serrations. There is also no extractor since the low adhesion of the .25 round allows the fired case to blow out without this part—altogether, a remarkable design.

Two flat springs are used, but only one of these causes trouble to any degree. The trigger guard is formed of tempered flat stock and also serves to tip the barrel upward when it is released. The other blade-type spring powers the barrel latch lever and on some of these guns also retains the magazine. On this type, the magazine floorplate has lateral wings which lock into recesses in the grip frame and are held in place by frontal pressure on

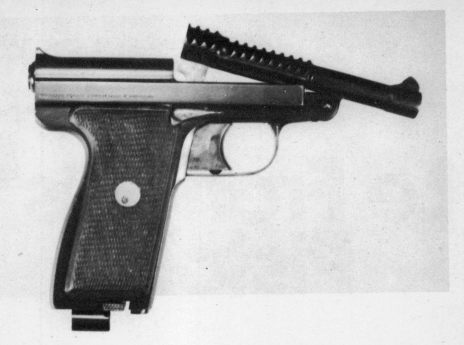

Right side of the 9mm Le Français Model 1928, showing the barrel tipped upward for loading. Loop on bottom of magazine floorplate has spring to hold spare round in readiness.

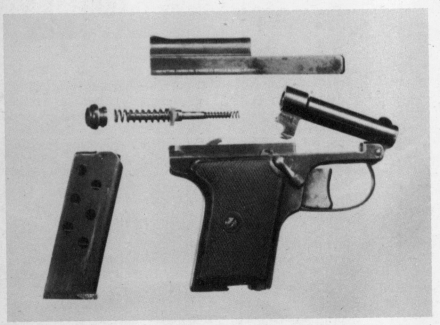

A field-stripped .25 Le Français. Note the solid striker with both main and rebound springs in place. Breakage of the striker is uncommon.

the magazine by this spring. The wings can be manually disengaged from the frame against the spring pressure, or the barrel can be released, taking the tension away from the spring to free the magazine. Many of these guns have a conventional pivoting magazine catch at the lower rear of the grip frame—a more efficient system. I have never seen a case of breakage of the trigger guard/barrel spring. The other one, however, is flexed rather severely, and breakage is not uncommon. A replacement is not particularly difficult to make, but unless your gunsmith is very familiar with these little guns, you had best try to save the broken parts for a pattern, as the exact length and curve are very important to proper operation. In regard to parts of any sort, Manufrance is still very much in business but is currently without a U.S. importing agent, so any inquiry would have to be sent directly to St. Etienne.

Original grips were of molded hard rubber, secured by a single screw on each side. In case of breakage, replacements will have to be handmade, as these have not been commercially reproduced.

In 1928, the same basic design was scaled up to a military-sized pistol, chambered for the 9mm

The 6.35mm Le Français Pocket Model shown has the wing-type magazine catch. Note the absence of slide serrations.

Browning Long cartridge with the hope of a government contract. This pistol was tested by the French Army, but was not adopted, and after limited commercial production, it was discontinued around 1938.

In 1950, Manufrance began producing a middle-sized model in 7.65mm (.32 auto) chambering, but this one was not exported to the U.S. and is seldom seen here. I would be inclined to sign the standard contract with Lucifer, in blood, to get one of these!

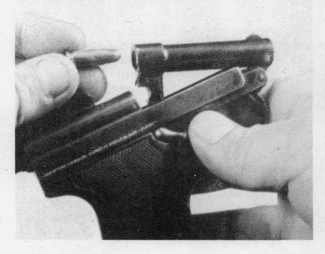

A lever on the right side of the frame tips the barrel up for loading or unloading the chamber.

Spanish Revolver

(Above) This "Spanish Revolver" is one of the better quality copies of the American S&W. It was made by Garate, Anitua and Company.

During the years between WW I and WW II, it would seem that every back room in Eibar, Spain, housed a small gun factory. Most of the handguns made in these fly-by-night operations ranged in quality from just fair to abysmally poor and gave Spanish arms in general a bad name. This was unfortunate, because several of the Spanish makers, even the lesser ones, continued to turn out guns of good quality. One of these was Garate, Anitua y Compania of Eibar, the maker of the revolver that is shown here. It is fairly typical of the type produced in this period. Most of these guns were close copies of the Smith & Wesson Model 10, the old standard Military & Police revolver, with one main difference. In the Spanish guns, the mainspring system was closer to the Colt pattern, with a large V-shaped blade spring supplying power to the hammer, cylinder hand and trigger.

These springs break with some regularity, and at one time Stoeger kept a stock of replacements on hand in various sizes. Dixie Gun Works still has some on hand, but in all cases a good deal of hand-fitting is required. I usually repair these guns by installing separate springs to power the parts. By cutting a slot in the lower inside edge of the grip frame, a Smith & Wesson Model 10 hammer spring can be adapted to function. In some cases, I have made a heavy round-wire spring, attached to the inside of the frontstrap of the grip frame, to power the cylinder hand and trigger.

On the Garate, Anitua y Compania revolver shown, I went even further by separating the alteration into three springs. I installed a new hammer spring, a coil spring and plunger inside the trigger, and used a coil spring and plunger in the sideplate to power the cylinder hand, in a manner similar to one of the early Smith & Wesson revolvers. This particular alteration is not always possible, as some of these guns have triggers that lack the necessary dimensions. In regard to the hammer spring, it is sometimes necessary to also add a strain screw in the lower frontstrap to increase the tension.

Broken firing pins are also a frequent problem, and these are usually a separate part, cross-pin-

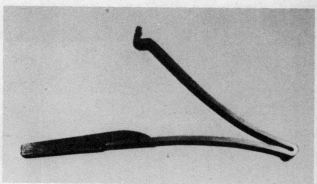

One of the V-shaped mainsprings commonly used in the Spanish revolvers. Hooks at top contact the hammer stirrup, while the flat arm at lower left enters a shelf on the cylinder hand to power the hand and trigger.

The two arrows at left indicate the Smith & Wesson Model 10 mainspring, adapted to the Spanish revolver. Arrow at right points to the location of a coil spring and plunger, installed in the trigger.

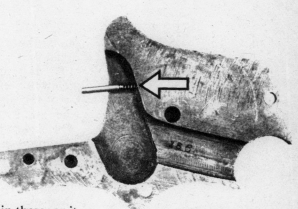

Sideplate of the Spanish revolver was drilled to accept a very small coil spring and plunger to power the cylinder hand.

ned to the hammer in Smith & Wesson style. In many cases, the Smith & Wesson firing pin can be adapted to these guns, but the inside contour and the pin hole will often have to be changed. The same can be said for the cylinder stop, especially in those that have followed the Model 10 pattern rather closely.

Some are such close copies that it is even possible to adapt Smith & Wesson grip panels to replace those that are broken. These guns will be found in several different chamberings, but one of the most popular was the .32-20 Winchester. Another chambering often seen is .38 Long Colt, and some of these, having straight-bored cylinders, will accept .38 Special rounds. Needless to say, none of the currently-made heavy police loads should be used in these, or it could be hazardous to your health.

For parts other than those that can be adapted, the only recourse would be the used-parts dealers.

Bernadelli Model 80 Pistol

The first of these well-made Italian guns began to be imported in quantity by several agents around 1973. It is available in .32 and .380 centerfire versions, but the majority of those sold in the U.S. are in the .22 Long Rifle chambering. The maker has long been known for producing quality arms, as Vincenzo Bernadelli founded the company in 1865, and the firm has been in continuous operation since that time. Beginning in 1945 a series of hammerless striker-fired automatic pistols in several sizes and calibers were put into production—all based on the same mechanical design. A .25 was made first, followed in 1947 by a .32 and .380 version, and in 1949 the .22 Long Rifle Standard Model appeared. Ten years later, in 1959, an entirely new model was offered, designated the Model 60. This gun with slight modification evolved into the currently-made Model 80.

In the .32 and .380 versions, the Model 80 has twin spring-powered buffers on the frame to cushion the slide impact. The mild recoil of the .22 doesn't need these, and they are omitted on the rimfire model. There are two separate manual safety systems—a Walther-style hammer block on the slide, and a sear/trigger block type on the frame. A fully adjustable rear sight is provided as standard equipment, and the gun has excellent balance and outstanding accuracy for a pistol of this size. The .22, which we are mainly considering here, does not have any chronic feed or ejection problems.

The only difficulty I have encountered with these guns involves the hammer-block safety. This unit operates in a manner very similar to the Walther, but there are differences. Rather than a square-shouldered internal blocking surface on the firing pin, there is a rounded swell on the Bernadelli pin, a less positive arrangement. Also, the cross-piece of the safety does not seem to be as tightly fitted to the slide, allowing a very slight fore-and-aft movement of the entire unit. Thus, even though the firing pin is held firmly by the safety, the pin and safety together can move a small distance when struck by the hammer. Pin length is the critical point here. If the firing pin is just a tiny bit too long, accidental firing is a possibility. I have seen two examples of this, which were easily corrected by a very slight shortening of the firing pin. This must be done very carefully, though, as taking off just a fraction too much can cause chronic

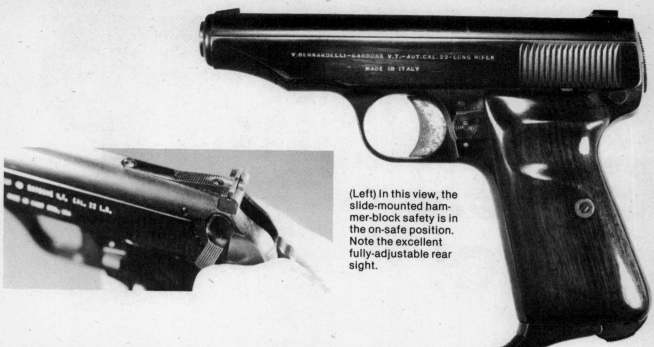

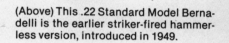

(Left) In this view, the slide-mounted hammer-block safety is in the on-safe position. Note the excellent fully-adjustable rear sight.

(Above) This .22 Standard Model Bernadelli is the earlier striker-fired hammerless version, introduced in 1949.

misfiring. When you consider the large numbers of this pistol in use today, I don't feel that these few isolated cases are an indictment of the design. It might, however, be a good idea to have your Bernadelli checked by a good gunsmith.

In most cases the Model 80 has grips of a tough modern plastic, in a style that extends around the rear of the grip frame to form the backstrap. These do not often break in normal use, but removal should be done very carefully. In the event of breakage, grips and other parts are readily available from any of several importers.

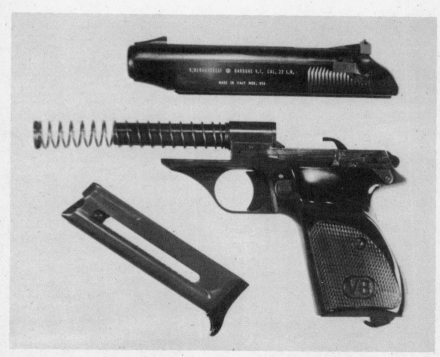

The Model 80 field-strips into three components: the slide, magazine and frame assembly.

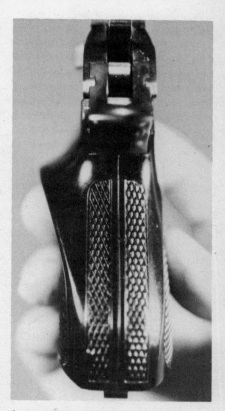

A rear view, showing how the grips meet at the rear to form the backstrap. After the screws are removed, they must be pried apart gently with a knife blade to avoid breakage.

Armi Galesi Pistol

This Armi Galesi pistol is in 6.35mm (.25 auto), but .22 caliber guns were also made.

Back in the days before our leaders, in their wisdom, decided that we could not be trusted with small imported pistols, the little .22 and .25 Galesi automatics were a familiar sight in most gunshops. There were several close imitations made at the time, one of which even had the Galesi name, but the quality piece was the one made by Industria Armi Galesi of Collebeato (Brescia) Italy. Nicola Galesi founded the firm in 1910, and it is now headed by his son, Giuseppe Galesi. The pistol with which we are familiar was originally designed and patented in 1930 and has continued with very little change until the present time. In 1950 it was designated "Model 9," and was imported into the U.S. in large numbers prior to 1968.

The Galesi is a true hammerless, striker-fired pistol and seems to break strikers with no more frequency than other guns of this type. The .22 version with its offset firing pin point does have more tendency to chip off. Fortunately, parts are still available. The striker spring base, which slides out to the rear for takedown, has been known to snap off at its narrowed portion, but this does not occur with any great frequency.

The sear and disconnector sys-tem is of unusual design, and while breakage is not a problem, their engagement with the trigger bar is quite delicate. Any wear or damage-through-tampering can be difficult to repair, and realignment is not a job for the amateur. The trigger bar lies in a narrow recess on the left side of the frame, and when the slide is removed, care should be taken that it doesn't fall out, as the slide holds it in place.

Although the Galesi is well-made of good materials, the heat-treatment level of the extractors

A rare sight—an unchipped and un-broken Galesi grip panel. They are very easily broken.

Arrow indicates the extractor which on some Galesi pistols is found to be lacking in hardness.

In the Galesi the trigger bar (arrow) lies in a narrow recess on the left side of the frame. With the slide removed, it can fall out and be lost.

seems to have been inconsistent. This extractor has a relatively long, thin beak, and I have seen numerous cases where the beak has struck the rim of the cartridge and been bent back against the breech face. In similar fashion, the tail of the extractor, which bears on the spring, will often bend outward. This lessens the compression of the extractor spring and allows the beak to slip off the rim of the case, causing the pistol to jam. Extractors may often be reworked and properly hardened, but even if this is not possible, replacements are available.

The original grips, which are usually either black or imitation pearl with a silver-colored "AG" medallion near the top, are made of a resin-based plastic which is very prone to chipping and breakage. The good news on this is that the commercial grip-makers have produced this one, and the replacements you buy will be better than the originals.

Even though they've been banned from importation for the past 10 years, these neat little guns are here in quantity and are frequently encountered. They are good quality guns, but be sure to check the points listed above.

The arrow points to the narrowed portion of the striker spring base, where breakage will occasionally occur.

The arrow indicates the interlocked sear and disconnector. Breakage is no problem, but the engagement is rather delicate.

Beretta Model 950B Pistol

From around 1950 to 1968, there were two neat little Beretta pistols available in the U.S., the smallest in their line. Unfortunately, they can't be imported now. The factory designation is Model 950B, but the .22 Short version was sold in the U.S. as the "Minx," while the .25 auto chambering was called the "Jetfire."

These nice little guns have several notable features. One of these had appeared earlier on the 1908 Steyr, the Jo-Lo-Ar and the Le Francais, and the system as used comes closest to the last named. The trigger guard is a heavy flat spring, bearing on the front-hinged barrel, and when a lever on the left side is moved, the rear of the barrel flips up for loading, unloading or cleaning. There is actually no need to manually draw back the slide, as the last round can simply be dropped into the chamber, and the barrel pushed back down into place.

Another interesting point is that the pistol has no extractor but relies on the low adhesion of the .25 auto and .22 Short cartridges, allowing the case to be blown back against the ejector without mechanical assistance. It works perfectly. Jamming in one of these little guns is rare and can nearly always be traced to bad ammo or deformed feed lips on the magazine from being dropped or otherwise damaged.

On the earliest guns, the slide was returned by two separate recoil springs of square-section stock in a modified V-shape, located on each side under the grip panels, and keyed into recesses in the lower edge of the slide. This arrangement was later changed to a single torsion-type spring of heavy round wire, mounted on a cross-pin just behind the trigger, with two arms which looped to the rear and back up to contact the slide notches. There were a few cases of breakage with the early square-section springs, and this is probably the reason for the change. In the earlier pistol, (Model 950) there was a separate spring for the barrel latch. In the 950B the looped opposite end of the recoil spring performs this function.

The recoil spring of the 950B never breaks, but its slide-contact arms have been known to weaken after long use. When this happens, it is sometimes possible to reshape them and restore the tension, but replacements are available, as are all other parts.

In both the .22 and the .25 pistols, the firing pin is a full-reach,

The tempered trigger guard extends upward (arrow) to be the barrel tip-up spring.

non-inertia type, and it is unsafe to carry them with the chamber loaded and the hammer fully down. There is a safety step on the hammer which keeps it elevated slightly from the firing pin head, and this should definitely be used.

The original grips are of good quality plastic and seldom break, but they are susceptible to warping at the front if subjected to long periods of extreme heat, such as a car glove compartment or a fishing tackle box in the summer sun. Because of this, some owners of the Model 950B frequently replace the original grips with handmade panels of wood or some other material less affected by heat. If this is done, the grip-maker must proceed with caution. The original grips are carefully designed so that the stabilizing projections on the inside surfaces will clear the arms of the recoil spring during their arc when the pistol is fired. I recently examined a Model 950B which had beautiful staghorn grips, and the maker had studded their inside surfaces with numerous little steel pins to prevent rotation of the grips. Unfortunately, two of these on each side were right in the way of the sweep of the recoil spring arms, and they were badly deformed on the first shot.

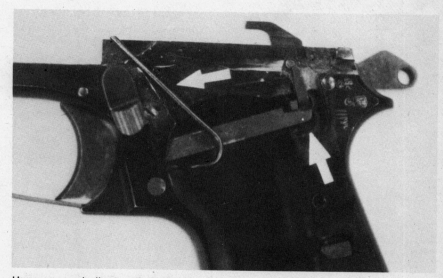

Upper arrow indicates the left arm of the torsion-type, round-wire recoil spring. Lower arrow points to the engagement of the trigger bar and sear.

Simple takedown of the Model 950B is very easy. Remove the magazine and trip the barrel latch. Lift the barrel straight up beyond its normal opened position. Cock the hammer, and lift the front of the slide until it clears its stop shoulder on the front of the frame, then move it slightly forward to free it from the ends of the recoil spring arms, and lift it off the frame. When reassembling, be sure that the recoil spring ends are hooked into their recesses in the lower edge of the slide and push it back and down into place. For the non-gunsmith, this is as far as disassembly should be carried, and it's adequate for routine cleaning.

In recent years, Armi Beretta made a marvelous addition to the design of the Model 950B—a double-action trigger system! The new gun is designated the Model 20; however, it's unavailable in this country as a result of the GCA-68.

Beretta Model 948 Pistol

This pistol is the .22 caliber counterpart of the standard Italian Military pistol of 1934 with very few differences. The extractor was moved from the top of the slide to the right side, the grip panels are entirely of plastic, without the metal backing of the Military pistol, and the frame is made of duralumin (aluminum alloy).

The principal mechanical difference is the lack of a safety step on the hammer, which, coupled with a full-reach, non-inertia firing pin, makes a less-than-ideal situation. When the chamber is loaded, it is unsafe to carry the gun with the hammer fully down, as the firing pin point will rest directly against the rim of the cartridge. For chamber-loaded carrying, the only alternative is to leave the hammer at full-cock, and apply the manual safety. Since this is only a trigger-block type safety, the alternative also makes me a bit nervous. On my own Model 948, I altered the hammer to include a positive safety step, keeping the hammer slightly away from the firing pin head when at rest.

Like most Beretta pistols, the 948 is almost entirely free of any routine maintenance problems. My gun has fired many thousands of rounds, using every known brand of ammunition, with not a single malfunction. In the shop, I have occasionally replaced broken firing pins on these guns, but this is a part susceptible to eventual breakage in any firearm.

Since some people will often remove the grips during cleaning operations, there is one point in the design, shared with the Model 1934, which should be mentioned. Under the left grip, the trigger bar/disconnector piece contacts a flat plate which acts as a lever to move the sear. This plate/lever is retained by a large slotted screw with a hexagon-shaped head, and many shooters, finding it slightly loose, are inclined to tighten it. *Don't.* This will bind the sear lever and in some cases prevent replacement of the grip panel. On the inside of the grip, there is a recess which exactly fits the shape of the screw head. The proper adjustment is to bring the screw down very lightly snug, then back it out just enough to align the screw head properly with the recess in the grip.

The only other caution about the Model 948 is in regard to complete disassembly of the frame. In this operation, it is possible for the amateur to deform the combination trigger bar and disconnector, disturbing its alignment with the

Arrow points to the sear-lever retaining screw which is designed to be slightly loose. A recess in the grip keeps it in position.

The arrow indicates the recess in the left grip which fits the head of the sear-lever screw.

slide and sear lever. This can usually be corrected without parts replacement, but in the event parts are needed, they are still available from several sources.

Armi Beretta began manufacturing the Model 948 in 1947, and production ended in 1958, when it was replaced by a slightly redesigned version. I'm sorry it's no longer made, as someday I may manage to wear mine out, and then I'll want another.

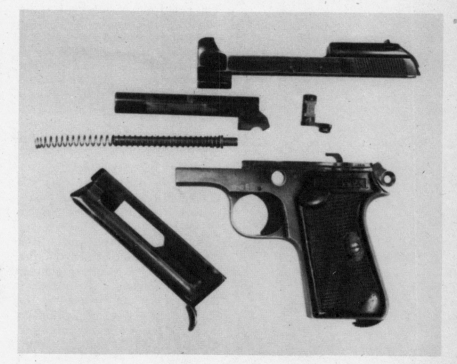

Field-stripping the Model 948 is fast and simple; however, any further disassembly of the frame is for professionals *only*.

Beretta Model 418 Pistol

This neat little .25 automatic is the only true hammerless, striker-fired design ever commercially produced by Beretta. It had its beginning in 1919 and was slightly redesigned in 1935 to become the Model 318. After WW II, in 1946, the grip panels and the shape of the grip safety piece were changed, and the pistol was designated the Model 418. In this form it was made until around 1958, when it was dropped in favor of the newer Model 950 pistol. The Model 418 was marketed in the U.S. prior to 1968 as the Beretta "Panther."

As with all of the designs of the late Signore Tullio Marengoni, the Model 418 is extremely simple, tough and reliable. Over the years I have repaired only two. One required only the replacement of the magazine (even a Beretta magazine will not survive being run over by an auto tire on a gravel road), and the other had a broken striker guide.

The striker in this gun is somewhat similar to the one used in the Mauser Model 1910 pistol, having an integral striker spring guide which also serves as a cocking indicator by protruding at the rear. I have seen one case in which the guide rod had broken away from the interior of the striker, deforming the spring and the tube-like secondary guide at the rear. When this occurs, it is not mechanically feasible to rejoin the guide to the body of the striker by welding. It is possible, though, to make a replacement guide with a collar at the forward end, press-fitting it in place within the striker. When this

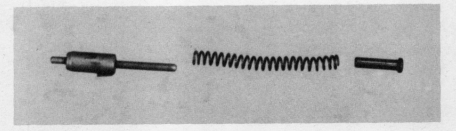

These are the parts of the striker system. The secondary guide at far right is a small, flanged tube and may be damaged if the main guide on the striker breaks.

Beretta Model 418, field-stripped. Note the striker assembly at right center. This is the only Beretta that does not have a pivoting hammer.

is done, it may also be necessary to shorten the spring by one or two coils to compensate for the space taken up by the collar. If the little tube-guide at the rear is damaged, a replacement can be made from brass tubing, available at hobby shops that carry materials for building model airplanes and trains. The Model 418 is of recent manufacture, and many parts sources still have parts for it in stock, so it may be possible to simply replace any broken part with a new one.

The firing system of this gun is of extremely simple design. The disconnector is a vertical projection on the trigger bar, and the bar makes direct contact with the heavy, solid sear. The manual safety lever blocks the movement of the trigger, and the grip safety acts directly on the sear. There is ample compensation for any wear that might occur, and nothing delicate that is likely to get out of adjustment. It would be possible, during amateur disassembly of the frame, to deform the trigger bar/disconnector piece, but this would not happen in normal operation.

Original grips are of molded microcell plastic and are not prone to breakage. If it should happen, replacements are available.

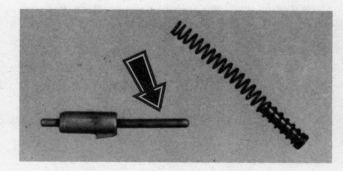

Arrow points to the main striker spring guide which also serves as a cocking indicator. If it breaks away from the striker body, it can damage the spring and the small tube at the rear.

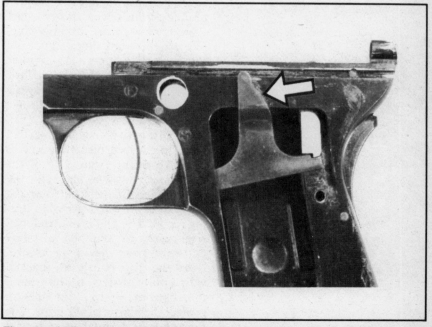

The arrow indicates the combination trigger bar and disconnector. It is susceptible to damage only during amateur disassembly.

Beretta Model 1934 Pistol

During his career as chief designer for Armi Beretta, Signore Tullio Marengoni produced many distinguished engineering accomplishments and before his death was awarded the title of Maestro del Lavoro, the highest honor for an Italian engineer. In my own opinion, his greatest triumph was the Beretta Model 1934. Here is a medium-sized holster pistol in which every point of the design is exactly right. It doesn't have a double-action trigger system, and there is no separate hold-open device when the last shot is fired, but this is all the criticism that anyone could manage. Every part is a little heavier and stronger than necessary, and the incidence of chronic parts breakage is zero.

Its distinctive magazine extension, the curved piece that comes down from the front edge of the floorplate, gives a place for all three fingers on the frontstrap and helps to control muzzle whip during recoil. The gun is all machined steel with no stamped or alloy parts and seems heavy for its size. Even the grip panels are backed with a plate of steel, rolled around the edges at the top and sides to protect the plastic of the grips. The firing pin, if original, is an inertia type, and the hammer also has

a safety step. The manual safety blocks only the trigger and must be swung through a 180-degree arc between the on-safe and off-safe positions. For those with a short thumb, less ape-like than mine, this can be awkward. With the external hammer, though, the only time the manual safety is needed is to lock the slide open for take-down.

This, incidentally, is extremely easy. With the magazine out, set the safety lever in the on-safe position and draw the slide back until it locks open. Then, push the barrel straight to the rear until it clears its tracks in the frame and lift the barrel up and out at the rear. Next, hold onto the slide, release the safety, and run the slide forward off the frame. Some barrels will be tight and must be tapped on the muzzle with a non-marring tool such as a plastic hammer or screwdriver handle. When the slide is off and the recoil spring and guide removed, the safety is free to drop out of the frame, so be careful it doesn't become lost.

The magazines are particularly well-made, with a full-shroud machined-steel follower to take the shock of acting as a hold-open on the last shot. The sides of the magazines are open, and after the

The sear-lever retaining screw (arrow) is somewhat "loose" under normal conditions—*don't* tighten it!

first two rounds are loaded, the follower can be grasped with the fingers, making it easy to load the rest. The magazine floorplate is retained by the hole-and-lockplate method, and disassembly for cleaning is not difficult, but be careful not to lose the lockplate.

Under the left grip is a flat pivoting plate retained by a hexagonal-headed screw, and this is the lever that transmits motion from the trigger bar to the sear. Many people, on taking off the left grip, and finding this screw to be slightly loose, will proceed to tighten it. Wrong. There is a recess inside the grip panel which matches the shape of the screw head, and the right adjustment is to bring the screw down just barely snug, then back it off until the head fits the recess in the grip panel. If it's too tight, it will bind the sear lever, and everything stops.

The Model 1934 is actually a combination of several of Marengoni's earlier designs, taking the best features from the Models 1915, 1923, and 1931 pistols. Its cartridge, called the 9mm Corto (9mm Short) in Italy, is the same as our .380 auto. Beginning in 1935, the gun was also made in 7.65mm (.32 auto). Production of the gun in both calibers ended in 1958,

when the gun was redesigned to become the "70 Series," in .22, .32, and .380 calibers, with a streamlined grip frame and other changes. These Model 70 pistols are excellent guns, but the old Model 1934 somehow just feels better in my hand.

In the unlikely event that something breaks, most parts are still available from several sources.

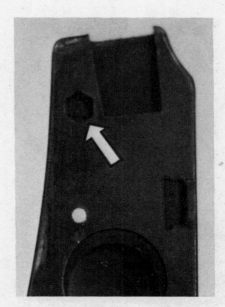

Arrow points to the hexagonal aperture in the steel sheathing of the left grip, which fits the head of the sear-lever screw.

Beretta Model 951 Pistol

This was Signore Tullio Marengoni's final design, and it was sold commercially as the "Brigadier." The "951" designation is simply the last three digits of its date of design—the year 1951. Beretta's first heavy-caliber, locked-breech pistol, the Model 951 was soon adopted as military standard by Italy, Egypt, and Israel, with the military pistols differing very slightly from the commercial version. The balance and other handling qualities of this gun are superb, and it delivers outstanding accuracy. It has even entered the world of fiction, in Don Pendleton's well-written "Executioner" series, with hero Mack Bolan blasting the Mafia with his "Beretta Belle."

The locking system of the Model 951 is a modified version of the one originally used in the Walther P-38 pistol, a vertically swinging block on the underside of the barrel with side wings that lock into recesses in the slide. These recesses, machined upward from the lower edges of the slide, almost extend to the outside top of the side rails, leaving a very thin section to cover them. The thin portion is under no strain, and there is ample steel in the necessary areas, but the nearness of the cuts to the top of the slide rails has given rise to stories about the slide cracking in that area. I have heard the stories, but I have never seen a single slide cracked in this way or even a photo of one. I can't positively say that it hasn't happened, or won't happen, but weigh this: The Model 951 is the standard side arm for three armies, two of which have used the gun in combat situations (with each other!). After more than 10 years of use, it is still their official weapon. Italy has rather rigorous proof testing, and each one of these pistols is subjected to firing with a proof load that creates pressures 30 to 50 per cent higher than the heaviest commercial load. Finally, my own Brigadier has been fired more than 1,000 times with not the slightest problem and

One of the two locking lug recesses in the slide (arrow). The thin section above these gave rise to stories of cracking.

Unlike earlier Beretta pistols, the Model 951 has a separate disconnector, dovetail-mounted on the right side of the frame.

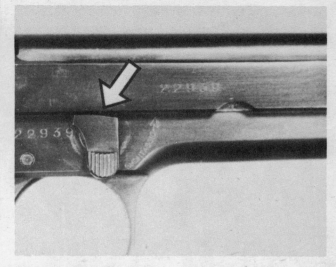

The takedown latch (arrow) is located on the right side of the 951's frame.

the cartridges have included some rather vicious handloads and custom loads.

The Model 951 has a takedown system that is so quick and easy it seems almost magical to the onlooker who is unfamiliar with it. With the magazine removed, you just draw back the slide until a semi-circular cut in its lower edge aligns with the takedown lever on the right side of the frame, flip the lever up and forward, and run the slide, barrel, and recoil spring assembly forward off the frame. It should be noted that the takedown lever is held in the frame by friction only, depending on the tension of a circular round-wire spring in a groove in its pivot shaft. It will not fall out, but can easily be nudged or jarred out of its hole in the frame—care should be taken that it isn't lost.

On several Model 951 pistols I have examined, the rear edge of the hammer recess in the frame was as sharp as a knife, a situation that becomes very apparent if the thumb slips while cocking. On my own gun, a few strokes with an India stone soon cured this. There is a safety step on the hammer, but the firing pin is an inertia type, and carrying it with the chamber loaded and hammer fully down is

quite safe. The manual safety is unusual, of a type rarely used on a handgun, but common on rifles and shotguns. It is a push-button, cross-bolt type, directly blocking the sear. On the commercial pistol, the magazine release is also a push-button, located in the lower rear corner of the left grip panel. All of the springs in the Model 951 are of round wire, either helical coil or shaped otherwise according to function. There are no parts that are chronically susceptible to breakage.

Original grips are of good-quality microcell plastic, meeting at the back of the handle and retained by a single screw on each side. They are undercut at the front edge to lock into the frame, and removal must be done carefully. After taking out the screws, pry them gently apart at the rear, using a knife blade or a similiar thin tool.

As you may have gathered by now, the Brigadier is one of the very good ones.

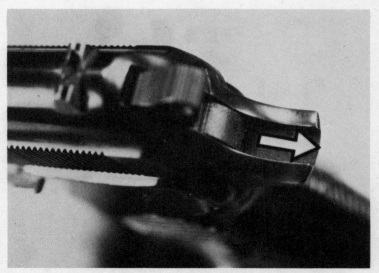

Arrow points to the rear edge of the hammer recess in the frame. On some pistols, this edge is knife-sharp.

Webley Revolver

This Webley (above) is the .38 caliber Mark IV Model. The S&W .38 round is nearly identical with its British cousins and will fire without a hitch in the Mark IV.

The classic British Service revolver is as rugged as a truck (perhaps we should say "lorry?"), and hardly anything ever goes wrong with it. All of the parts are a little heavier than absolutely necessary, and breakage rarely occurs.

The mainspring, which powers the hammer, cylinder hand, and trigger, is a heavy V-type leaf spring, and it is fully flexed during the firing cycle. Although blade springs are more prone to breakage than the round-wire type, I have never seen a Webley with a broken mainspring.

In fact, the only repair I've ever done on the Webley is replacement of the barrel latch spring, and this not often. Unlike most early U.S. top-break revolvers, the Webley has a very strong and positive barrel lockup. There is a vertical rectangular projection from the top of the frame which fits tightly into an opening at the rear of the barrel extension. There is a pivoting latch which sits astride the top of the frame with its left arm extended downward to form a thumb lever. The shorter arm of the latch, on the right side of the gun, bears on a heavy little V-type blade spring which is mounted on the back of the recoil shield. When the barrel latch is operated, this spring is ful-

ly compressed, and occasionally one of these will snap. Replacement springs are available from several of the used-parts suppliers, but installation is not a job for the amateur.

I would like to pass along a word of caution in regard to the early .455 Webleys. They were designed for a black powder cartridge, and the frames and barrel latches of these older guns were not made to take the pressure of modern smokeless loads. When the

The arrow points to the flat V–type spring that powers the Webley's barrel latch—the only thing on this gun that occasionally breaks.

Originally made in .455 caliber, this big Webley Mark VI revolver has had the rear face of its cylinder altered to accommodate the .45 ACP and auto-rim rounds.

Webleys were being sold as surplus a few years ago, several importers and dealers machined off the rear face of the cylinders to allow the use of .45 automatic cartridges in half-moon clips or .45 auto-rim rounds. Both of these have a higher breech pressure than the original black powder load and should not be used in the older converted guns. No problem with the late Mark VI guns, as they were made for smokeless loads. The Webley bores are a true .455, and the two rounds mentioned above are .450 diameter. While the lead-bullet .45 auto-rim will upset enough to fill the rifling, the full-jacketed .45 automatic bullet barely touches the lands, and intended targets have to be very close, and very large.

With the .38 Mark IV Webley, there are no cartridge problems, as our standard .38 S&W round is nearly identical with the British cartridge. The .38 S&W has a lighter bullet, and for serious target work you will probably have to change the front sight blade, as the point of impact differs.

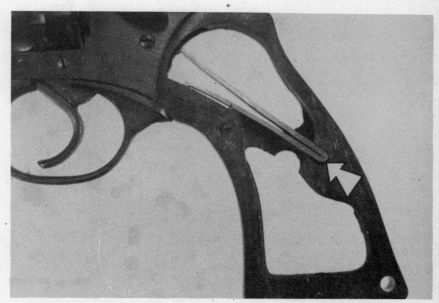

The Webley's mainspring (arrow) is a blade-type, V-shaped spring. Although flexed severely, it seldom breaks.

Webley Automatic Pistols

The Webley .455 pistol shown above is the Mark I No. 2 version (with slot for a shoulder stock) as issued to the Royal Flying Corps in 1915.

The name "Webley" brings to mind many scenes, all of them very British—Gordon at Khartoum in the steaming Sudan—a British commando with cork-blackened face—Sherlock Holmes' colleague, Dr. Watson, and his infamous Webley. In all of these scenes, the gun you have in mind is probably the familiar British revolver. You may be unaware that Webley & Scott also produced a line of fine automatic pistols. With minor variations, they were all based on one original design, patented in 1903 by W.J. Whiting, a Webley design engineer.

The calibers ranged from the monstrous .455 down to the diminutive .25, and in between were the .38 auto, 9mm Browning Long, 9mm Browning Short (.380 auto), and 7.65mm Browning (.32 auto). Regular production spanned from 1904 to 1940, but not all of the calibers were continuously made. The single departure from the original pattern was the second model of the .25 Webley which had a coil-type recoil spring. Since this one was made in very small quantity and is not likely to be encountered often, let's concentrate on the pistols of standard pattern.

In these, the recoil spring is a large, heavy V-blade, located inside the right grip panel—it bears on a lever which contacts a recess in the slide. When you consider the severe flexing this spring receives with each shot, it is amazing that so few of them break. I have observed *one* broken recoil spring over the years, that one in a .32 Webley. Because of the moderate power of the .32 auto round, it was possible to form a replacement from heavy round wire. In the larger calibers, this solution might not be feasible, and original parts are virtually impossible to find.

With the slide partially removed, and the barrel lifted partway from its enclosure, the angled locking lugs can be seen. The system is similar to the Blish design, used in early models of the Thompson submachine gun.

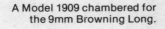

The Model 1909 strips into four basic elements. Note the "unsprung" trigger guard—the key to the takedown.

A Model 1909 chambered for the 9mm Browning Long.

The takedown system of the .455 and .38 pistols, while not difficult, is somewhat involved and does require several separate steps. In the lesser calibers, it is both simple and easy. Pulling the tempered bow of the trigger guard forward will jump its lower end out of a recess in the grip frame and allow the barrel and slide to be run forward off the frame. The magazine, of course, has already been removed before starting the takedown. Although the trigger guard is, in effect, a blade-type spring, it is a heavy one and is not severely flexed in the unlocking process. Breakage is unlikely.

The recoil spring and the trigger guard are the only flat springs in the design, all of the others being helical coil round wire. The internal parts are all made with an ample allowance for strength, and there is nothing delicate about the Webley pistols. Mr. Whiting's mechanical design is totally unlike most other automatics which follow the Browning pattern, and even a gunsmith who is familiar with basic automatic design might occasionally be a bit confused. In other words, complete disassembly and attempted repair by the amateur is definitely not recommended.

The manual safety was made in several variations, but on most of the pistols the safety was a lever at the top of the left grip panel. When pushed upward, it cammed the trigger bar out of engagement with

Located inside the right grip panel, this massive V-spring and lever are the recoil system of the .455 pistol. The smaller calibers use a similar arrangement.

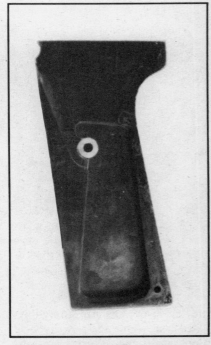

In this view you can see the right grip panel of the .455, showing the inside hollowed area for the spring and lever —breakage is not unusual.

Most of the Model 1913 pistols were made in 7.65mm (.32 auto), but a smaller number were made in .380 auto.

Of interest is the grip safety system of the .455—it is very efficient. The arrow indicates the sear lever. Note how it is solidly blocked by the frame (top photo) with the safety out, and given clearance to move when the safety is depressed (bottom photo).

the sear lever. The grip safety, provided on some models, is even more positive. When it is not depressed, the sear rests solidly against a shoulder in the frame and cannot be moved by any reasonable force.

Although the commercial model of the 1909 pistol in 9mm Browning Long was supplied with walnut grips, most of the pistols had grip panels of molded hard rubber. With the right grip being extensively hollowed for the recoil spring

and lever, and the left one cut out for the safety lever, breakage is not unusual. No commercially-made replacements have been manufactured.

The fit and finish of these pistols is superb, and the design used no stamped parts. They were made with much hand-fitting, in the old English tradition, and could not survive at a competitive price in this modern manufacturing age. Like the Luger and the Mauser Military Pistol, they became anachronisms, and the start of WW II marked their demise. I lament their passing, as this was one of the most mechanically perfect designs ever made.

Colt Single-Action Army Revolver

If you discount the lapse between 1941 and 1955, this gun can claim the longest production period of any commercially made cartridge handgun—from 1873 until the present time. It has been known by many names, being called the Single Action Army, Frontier Six-Shooter, Peacemaker, and the factory designation, Model "P." During its early years of production, it was chambered for a long list of cartridges, but the most prevalent chamberings were for the .45 Colt, closely followed by the .44-40 and .38-40, both of which would interchange with the Winchester rifle, thus solving the logistic problems of the cowboy in the far places. The long success of this gun was due not only to its rugged dependability, but also to the fact that it was easy to repair under conditions that could, in those days, be fairly primitive.

With the jarring fall of its large, heavy hammer and its atrocious sights, accuracy was a sometime thing. Fortunately, it was seldom called upon for any medium to long-range target work, as it was chiefly employed as an instrument of peace and non-violence. When an old-time law officer or law-abiding citizen found it necessary to haul out the big Colt, the offending bad guys soon became very peaceful and non-violent. The ranges involved were usually no more than three or four yards, and for this the accuracy was quite adequate.

The arrow indicates the operating surface of one of the ratchet planes on the cylinder. Extreme wear here is a real problem, as the ratchet is integral with the cylinder.

The arrow points to the ejector return spring, one of the few helical coils used in this design—it is prone to weakening.

Most smokeless-powder guns, after serial number 165000, will have this spring-type base pin latch (arrow).

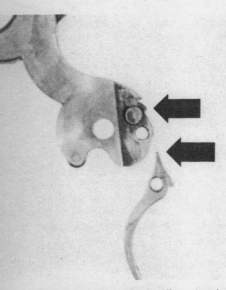

On this hammer, the loading step (upper arrow) has a broken lip—a dangerous situation. Top extension of the trigger (lower arrow), intact on this one, is also subject to breakage.

The Single Action is full of blade-type springs. In fact, the only helical coils are the ejector return spring, the loading gate spring and, on the later smokeless powder guns (above serial number 165000), the cylinder base pin latch spring. The heavy hammer spring is not prone to breakage, but the rest of them require replacement at one time or another if the gun sees much use. The cylinder hand spring breaks with some frequency, as does the single twin-armed spring that powers the trigger and cylinder stop (Colt calls this latter part the "bolt").

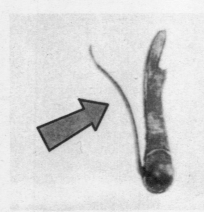

In the S.A.A. the cylinder hand is powered by a blade-type spring (arrow), and with normal use eventual breakage is to be expected.

The cylinder stop itself has two tempered tails, one of these acting as a spring when it is pushed aside by a stud on the hammer as the hammer falls. When replacement is necessary, the left wing of the new "bolt" must be hand-fitted to insure proper functioning.

The large, cone-pointed firing pin does not break often, but if it should, it can be replaced with very little difficulty by driving out its cross-pin and pushing the broken part forward out of the hammer face. There is even a small hole at the rear of the hammer to admit a drift for this purpose.

There are three steps on the front curve of the hammer, deep cuts for the safety and loading positions, and a narrower shelf for full-cock. The outer lip of the first two often shears off, and the old-timers soon learned to carry the gun with only five chambers loaded, keeping an empty under the hammer. If the loading step is broken, it is possible to recut it to a safe depth, but when this is done, the timing may also have to be slightly adjusted to compensate for the changed hammer position.

The narrow sear surface at the top extension of the trigger is also prone to breakage, and when this happens, it will not properly enter

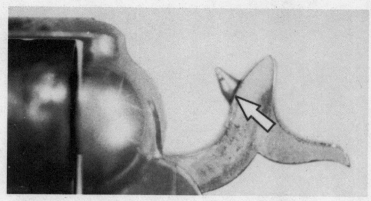

Colt's conical-point firing pin (arrow) rarely breaks, but if it should happen, it is easily removed and replaced.

the safety and loading steps on the hammer. The only real cure for this is replacement of the trigger. Parts are no problem at all—they are available everywhere.

In the old days, many different materials were used in making grips for the Single Action, but the most common factory-supplied grips were of either black hard rubber or mother-of-pearl. In both cases, these should be considered to be very fragile, especially the pearl. Perhaps this is why we see so many of these guns with grips of staghorn, bone and wood.

As old photos and records prove, the Old West saw the use of many other guns—the Remington, Smith & Wesson, and so on. The magic of the cinema, however, has convinced the average person that any cowboy who was worth a damn carried the Colt "hawg-leg." Thus are legends born.

Tensioned by a split blade spring (arrow), the trigger and cylinder stop are retained by a flat screw. The one shown is an old replacement, not original.

The cylinder stop, or "bolt," as Colt calls it, has thin tempered wings at the rear, the left one contacting a stud on the hammer. Breakage is an eventual certainty.

Colt Old Model .25 Automatic

The proper factory designation for this pistol is Model "N," but I thought that if it were titled that way only a few Colt collectors would know what we were talking about. So, I've called it the "Old Model," to distinguish it from the later .25 bearing the Colt name, which was actually an Astra Cub in disguise.

Designed by John Moses Browning in 1904/05, this pistol was first produced by the Fabrique Nationale in Belgium beginning in 1906. Browning soon leased the American manufacturing rights to Colt, and production began in this country on October 30, 1908, continuing until 1941. Unlike most Browning designs, which usually have a pivoting hammer, this little Colt is a true hammerless, striker-fired gun. Safety features are abundant. There is a manual safety lever which blocks the sear and locks the slide, and a grip safety which also blocks the sear. From serial number 141000 upward, there is a magazine safety which disconnects the trigger bar from the sear when the magazine is removed. As with most Browning designs, the internal mechanism is not complicated, and parts are not delicate or prone to breakage.

There is one blade spring in the design, a V-type located in the rear of the grip frame. Its longer front arm is split to form twin springs which power the sear and the trigger bar/disconnector. At the lower end of the grip frame, the shorter rear arm of the spring tensions the grip safety and, via a hole near the lower end, keys into the magazine catch. If one of these multi-directional jobs breaks, you are in trouble, as used parts for this gun are in short supply, and this spring has not been commercially reproduced.

This gun has no more incidence of firing pin breakage than any other of its type, but when it happens, the ailment is not serious. The original striker can be re-pointed by any competent gunsmith. Currently-made replacements are available. Also, you might keep in mind that this striker is identical to, and interchangeable with, the one used in the Browning 1910/22 pistols.

One part of this gun that is not tolerant to amateur gunsmithing is the striker spring base—the small doll's head shape that projects upward from the rear of the frame. In what must be fairly frequent occurrence, the person field-stripping the gun will leave the striker in cocked position. When the slide is

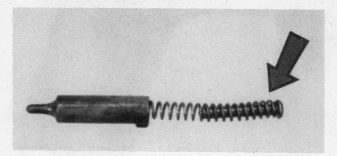

If the striker spring guide (arrow) is lost, the proper length of any replacement is a critical point.

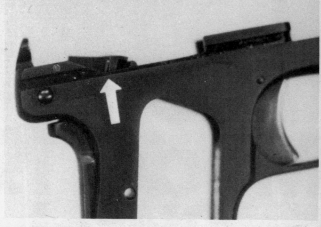

The upper right end of the combination sear and trigger bar spring is visible (arrow) where it contacts the sear. A V-blade type, its lower portion operates the grip safety and magazine catch.

run forward during removal and the striker is free of its tunnel, it will usually jump off the sear. The striker will often stay in the vicinity, but its spring and guide will zing away into infinity. Many people, when this happens, will install a makeshift spring and guide, and that's where the trouble begins. With the slide at full rearward travel, there is a certain minimum space between the front inside surface of the striker and the fixed spring base at the rear. Put in a spring that's a little too long, or a guide that's too long, and the spring base will be bent or broken on the first shot. It works the other way, too. A spring that's too short will cause misfiring, and a follower that's too short will cause the spring to be badly deformed. Therefore, when the striker spring and/or its guide are lost or damaged, leave replacement to a gunsmith. A good one.

On the earlier pistols the original grips will be of black molded hard rubber, retained by a single screw through the frame. These are prone to chipping and breakage and become especially brittle with age. Grips of genuine pearl were also available, and these should be considered fragile as glass. Later pistols had grips of checkered wal-

Field-stripped view shows the Colt Old Model 25 broken down into its basic component parts.

nut, and these are much more durable. Commercially made grips for this pistol are offered in many styles and materials.

Original, unaltered examples of the Model "N" in like-new condi-

tion are of great interest to Colt collectors, but most of these little pistols in ordinary condition are still being put to practical use as personal protection pieces.

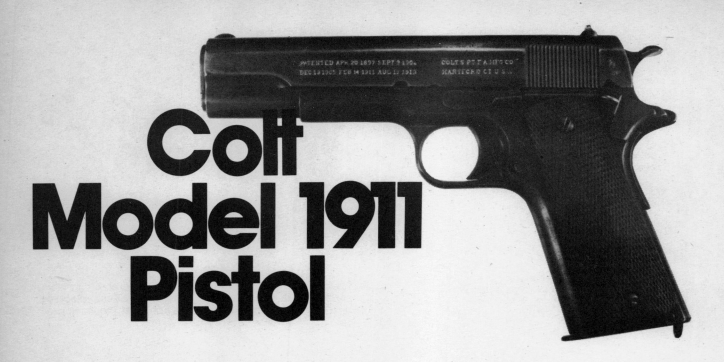

Colt Model 1911 Pistol

The Colt Model 1911 pistol shown above is the original version with straight mainspring housing, long trigger, and other small differences from the later 1911 A-1.

Since almost all shooters and military men are thoroughly familiar with the history of this gun, I think the usual background remarks can be omitted. It will be sufficient to point out, for the newcomers, that the original version had a straight-backed mainspring housing, a comparatively long trigger and grip safety extension, and a wide-spur hammer. The later 1911A-1 and the current commercial version have an arched, vertically grooved mainspring housing, a much shorter trigger, longer grip safety extension and a spur the same width as the hammer. The Commander, a relatively recent development, is shorter overall and has a European-style "ring" hammer. Chamberings are .45 auto, .38 Super auto, and 9mm Parabellum (Luger).

The reliability of this gun is almost legendary. You can submerge it in mud, sand or any other material that would stop most automatics, and it will simply continue to function, as it has through several wars. I think it is this, coupled with its cannon-sized projectile in the .45 chambering, which has helped an outdated design to retain its widespread popularity. In the full-sized military version, the pistol has all of the fine

hang and balance of an electric hand-drill, and its twisting recoil makes subsequent aimed shots require a gorilla-like grip. It is possible, of course, to shoot outstanding scores with this gun. Possible, but very difficult. The great John Moses Browning designed it. Some 20 years later, shortly before his death, he designed another large military pistol in which he corrected most of his earlier mistakes. This one emerged in 1935 as the Browning Hi-Power, but that's another story.

Regarding the mechanical aspects, there is not much room for criticism. It may be an ungainly beast, but it's a beast that *works*. There are two flat springs in the design, but neither is susceptible to breakage. The extractor is tempered to be its own spring, but this part is very heavy, and I've never seen one break other than a chipping of the beak when a manufacturing slip drew the heat treatment a bit too hard. The other blade-type spring is a long, three-fingered combination which powers the sear, trigger, disconnector, and grip safety. These rarely break, but after long use may show signs of weakening, especially the right-hand wing, which powers the grip safety. In most

In this bottom view of the slide, the arrow indicates the firing pin retainer, this one showing a small visible gap at its leading edge. This can cause a safety problem.

Arrow indicates the housing for the spring and plungers which supply tension for positioning of the safety and slide stop. The housing is riveted to the frame and is difficult to tighten.

cases, these springs can be reshaped, but most people just put in a new one, as parts are abundantly available and low priced.

The disconnector passes vertically through the sear, and the sear is somewhat skeletonized to allow for this. I have seen quite a few cases in which the sear had cracked, either at its upper and lower bridges or at the pivot point. For those brave souls who insist on carrying the Model 1911 "cocked and locked," this is something to think about.

With any pistol of this type, having an external hammer and an inertial firing pin, my preferred method of carrying it has always been to load the chamber, then gently let the hammer all the way down. The recent experience of a friend has caused me to rethink this one. With a Model 1911A-1 stuck in his belt, in the condition above, he caught a playfully pitched soft-drink bottle and brought it down quickly to his lower chest, like a football player tucking in a caught pass. The bottom of the bottle struck the spur of the hammer, which was fully down, and there was a very loud noise. He was very fortunate— only a flesh wound of the upper leg. But, how did it happen? The

This is the three-fingered, blade-type spring which powers the sear, trigger, disconnector and grip safety. These seldom break but are prone to weakening.

answer was ridiculously simple.

His gun was one of those creations, made up from surplus parts and using one of the currently-produced lightweight frames. All of the internal parts had been carefully hand-fitted with proper attention given to the safety and sear engagement, but who pays any attention to the firing pin retainer? And, if it has about three to five thousandths end play, what difference can it make? Apparently, a lot. Be sure that the firing pin retainer, or "stop," is tight, by whatever means necessary. There is enough variation in tolerances that this can often be achieved by simply substituting another retainer. Since the incident described above, I've carefully checked my own guns that have a similar system, by putting an empty primed

case in the chamber, letting down the hammer, and giving it a sharp rap with a nylon hammer head.

At the top of the left grip there is a little steel tunnel, the housing for the spring and two plungers which supply positioning tension to the slide stop and the manual safety lever. This housing is attached to the grip frame by two rivets which are spread into recesses inside the frame. Since the location of these is within the magazine well, they are extremely difficult to reach with a punch for tightening. Also, too much force will collapse the housing. Once, in a military ordnance shop, I saw a marvelous little tool which precisely fit the top of the magazine well with vertical punch heads that transferred the force to two lateral rods positioned exactly over the rivets. Tap, tap, and it was done. Unfortunately, stealing from a U.S. military installation is a federal crime, so I left it there. When this little housing loosens on your gun, proceed carefully or send it to Colt for factory tightening.

Old Model Colt Police Positive Revolver

(Above) Colt Police Positive revolver shown is the later redesigned gun. The old original model had a full-length grip frame with unrounded corners, narrower in the top section.

When you compare this small frame .38 to the heavy revolvers used by most of today's law enforcement officers, it seems strange to remember that guns of this type were once the standard side arm of many police forces. The Police Positive was introduced in 1908 and by 1928 was being used by so many law officers that the gun was slightly redesigned and designated the "Official Police" revolver. The original pattern "Police Positive," however, continued in production until 1947, and many of them are still in use today.

Although these guns were made with the usual Colt precision, many of the early ones have seen such long and continuous use that some trouble spots are beginning to show up. The cylinder stop (Colt calls it the "bolt") is not operated by direct contact with the trigger, as in most other revolvers. Instead, it is tripped at the rear by a corner of the rebound lever, the part which transfers power from the lower arm of the mainspring to the cylinder hand and trigger. If the rear projection of the cylinder stop loses its temper, or if the mating surfaces of the stop arm and the stud on the rebound lever are badly worn, the system will fail to

trip the stop and release the cylinder for rotation. If the wear isn't too severe, it's sometimes possible to recut the parts, and retemper the spring portion of the stop. If the stop is broken or too worn, it will have to be replaced. The last time I ordered these, the factory still had them in stock.

In the same area, another occasional trouble spot is the cylinder stop pivot screw. Its threaded portion is stepped down to a rather small diameter with very fine threads. If this screw is over-tightened, and the threads are stripped, the cylinder stop will be laterally loose and will not engage properly. If the frame threads are intact, a new screw can be installed. If not, a screw with a slightly larger threaded shank will have to be made, and the frame reworked accordingly.

The revolver has a hammer-block safety system which imposes a steel bar between the frame and the face of the hammer when the trigger is forward. The bar is connected to the trigger by a thin plate that Colt calls the safety lever, this part pivoting on the base of the hammer pivot. The connection to the trigger and safety bar is by very small pins which move in slots in the plate. If anything dis-

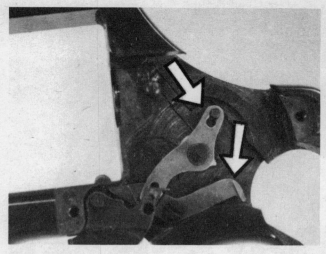

Upper arrow points to the safety bar at its connection with the flat plate-like lever that joins it to the trigger. Lower arrow indicates the spring-tempered rear arm of the cylinder stop.

O.M. Colt's ejector rod (arrow) is unprotected below the barrel. If the rod becomes bent, it can prevent rotation of the cylinder.

turbs these connections, the uncontrolled safety bar can jam the action. Care should especially be taken during disassembly and reassembly to see that the pins are in their slots.

The mainspring is a V-shaped blade-type, and although it is completely flexed in the firing cycle, it's rare for one of these to break. If it does happen, though, Colt can supply a new formed spring with a separate bracket and side stud to replace the original one-piece spring. Other parts are also available. A new cylinder hand is supplied with a little extra steel at the ratchet-contact surfaces to allow precise fitting and take-up of wear. The two-stage Colt hand system requires that this be done by a competent gunsmith.

The arrow points to the flat V-type mainspring. The one shown is the newer revised style. In earlier guns, the mainspring had an integral stud which keyed it into the frame.

Colt Python Revolver

Since its introduction in the late '50s, the Colt Python has become one of the world's most desired revolvers. No other gun, fresh out of the box from the factory, can match the smoothness of its double-action trigger pull, and its integral barrel weight gives the slight muzzle-heaviness that many serious shooters prefer. In an era when some hallowed names have turned out some things that are below their usual standard, the Python still shows outstanding quality in both materials and workmanship.

Like all revolvers, however, its lockwork does not have the ruggedness of most automatic pistols, and there are a few points that should particularly be watched to avoid trouble. As in any revolver, the timing is the heart of the action. With long, hard use, there can be wear or damage to the cylinder hand, cylinder ratchet, cylinder stop (some call it the "bolt") and to the stop slots in the cylinder. If the timing is not perfect, the cylinder will fail to align with the firing pin and barrel. The cylinder stop is the part under the most strain because it receives an impact with each turn of the cylinder. Its rear arm, which contacts a stud on the rebound lever, is

spring-tempered to snap back over the stud on the return of the lever when the trigger is released. Here again, any wear or chipping of the contact surfaces can be a trouble spot.

A faulty cylinder stop is no great problem though, as a new one can easily be obtained and installed. Most of the time, the replacement will require very little fitting. In the case of the other parts mentioned, however, these will usually require some fitting by a good gunsmith. If the ratchet steps are damaged or worn, it's back-to-the-factory time.

There are several revolvers that can be jammed by a bent ejector rod. In any gun which has an ejector rod that is rigidly attached to the ejector/ratchet and turns with it, any serious deformation will bring the rod against the barrel, or the sides of its well, stopping everything. In the Python, the ejector rod is well-protected deep within a heavy steep enclosure when the cylinder is locked in place. The rod itself, though, is very slim, and when the cylinder is opened for loading, the rod could be damaged if struck against a solid object or if the gun were dropped. I know of one police officer who, reloading in the heat of

The safety bar and lever must be handled with care, especially during disassembly and reassembly. Arrow indicates joining point of safety bar and lever.

Extreme wear at the point of engagement between cylinder hand and ratchet can interfere with proper cylinder indexing.

Proper engagement of the spring-tempered rear projection of the cylinder stop (arrow) and the rebound lever stud is critical to the Python's timing.

a serious social encounter, slapped the ejector rod of his gun and bent it so badly that the cylinder would not go back into the frame. Of course, this should not be taken as a condemnation of the Python—the man in the incident described is a large and strong individual, and under the circumstances might have damaged *any* revolver. The point is that a revolver, no matter how well-made, should be operated with a certain degree of care.

This also applies to swinging the cylinder out and back during reloading. Many of us have watched with great amusement the tough private detective or solider-of-fortune on TV and in films, as he flips the cylinder out with an audible *clack* and snaps it back with a reverse motion of the wrist. Each time it is swung out in this manner, to stop short as the crane shelf hits the frame, a serious strain is put on the crane, and it will eventually be misaligned. As the cylinder is forcefully swung back into the frame, the side of the ratchet strikes the edge of its well in the breech face, and if this is done often, the edge will begin to peen. As soon as a peened edge is raised, it will contact the heads of the cartridges and can cause a nasty jam. Again, this is not peculiar to the

Python, but also applies to several other revolvers.

There is one mechanism in the Python, and in other Colt revolvers with the exception of the Mark III series, that must be handled with care when the gun is disassembled. It is the hammer-block system (Colt calls it the "safety" and "safety lever"), which prevents accidental firing from an external blow on the hammer. This consists of a blocking bar connected to a very thin pivoting plate which lies in a shallow well to the right of the hammer on the inside wall of the frame. The plate is connected to the bar and the trigger by two tiny studs. If the plate becomes bent or the studs damaged, the firing system can lock up completely. Before tightening the sideplate screws, be sure everything is properly in its place.

As mentioned earlier, the single- and double-action trigger pull of the Python is usually superb, just as it comes from Colt. For those who are not satisfied with this, and want absolute perfection, a word of caution: Smoothing the trigger system of this gun is definitely not a job for the amateur. When honing the mating surfaces of the internal mechanism, it is easy for the non-professional to go too far, and

then it's new-parts time at more cost than you'd pay a gunsmith to do it right. All parts are, of course, available from Colt.

Actually, the only real complaint about the Python is that there never seems to be enough of them around to meet the demand.

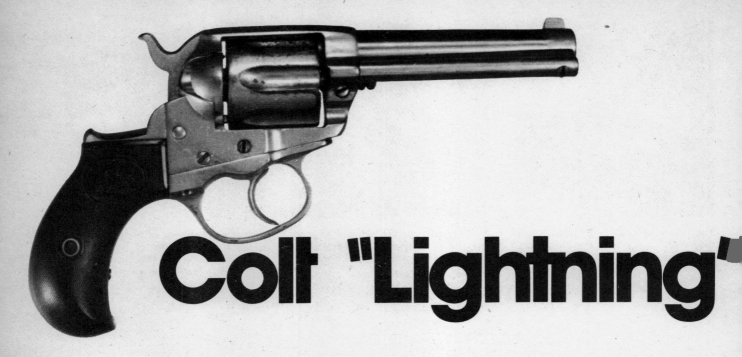

Colt "Lightning"

While he was employed by Colt, William Mason made several worthwhile contributions to that company's fine products. In 1876, though, he made a dreadful mistake. He designed their first double-action revolver. It was, and is, a total mechanical disaster. Considering the well-designed and finely made Colts which preceded and followed it, one wonders why it lasted until 1910. As most Colt collectors know, the names "Lightning" for the .38 and "Thunderer" for the .41 caliber were never Colt factory designations. These names were originated by B. Kittredge & Company of Cincinnati, Ohio, when these guns appeared in their catalog.

There are so many bad points in this design it's difficult to decide where to begin. Let's start with the cylinder stop, or "bolt," as some call it. This gun was designed with stop slots between the chambers on the rear face of the cylinder, rather than on the sides. The stop reaches the slots through a rectangular opening in the lower left corner of the breech face and in its operation must retract far enough and long enough to clear a portion of the cartridge head. To accomplish this the stop has a spring-tempered lower arm which is cammed up-ward by a stud on the trigger and is then allowed to slip off and drop back into place. As the trigger is released, the spring arm must flex outward to climb over the trigger stud and be ready for the next cycle. After it has done this for a certain unknown number of times, the spring arm breaks. Fortunately, new reproductions of this part are still being made, but these must be very carefully fitted. In due time, unfortunately, the new one will also break.

There is a separate sear for single-action firing, and it seems to have been added as an after-thought. It is sandwiched into a very small area between the trigger, hammer, and other parts, and its projections which contact the sear steps on the hammer are extremely thin. The engagement of the sear-trip arm with the trigger stud is a very precise adjustment, and this is lost with the first signs of wear.

The blade-type spring which powers the cylinder stop and sear has a shape so weird that it defies description. When one or both arms of this strange little spring break, and the usual parts sources are out of it, take a firm grip on something before you ask your gunsmith, "How much?"

Revolver

The trigger spring, a heavy blade-type, screw-mounted in the frame, contacts a roller on top of the trigger just a small distance to the rear of the pivot point. This gives very poor mechanical advantage and causes the spring to flex a great amount in proportion to its length. Breakage is frequent. The springs for the cylinder hand and hammer lever (called "trigger strut" in some parts lists) are two small blade-types, one atop the other, screw-mounted within the trigger. These, too, are quite fragile.

Throughout the gun, the engagement of all parts is very delicate with no margin for the slightest wear. It's been said that William Bonney favored the double-action Colt in .41 caliber. If Billy the Kid relied on one of these, Pat Garrett was never in any real danger.

Some newly made parts and some originals are available from Dixie Gun Works and Mrs. C.H. Weisz.

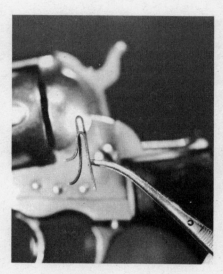

This is the strangely-shaped spring that powers the Lightning's cylinder stop and sear. It frequently weakens or breaks.

The forceps hold the Lightning's cylinder stop in the position it occupies when installed in the gun. The lower arm of this part is spring-tempered and relatively fragile.

Plainfield Model 71 Pistol

Designed by Gary Wilhelm, who was also responsible for the excellent Stoeger Luger .22 pistol, the Plainfield Model 71 was first marketed in May of 1973. It has a counterpart called the Model 72 which differs only in having a lightweight alloy slide and longer barrel. The Model 71 is entirely of stainless steel with a special surface plating called "Lube-Lock," a lubricating film permanently bonded to the steel. Both the Model 71 and Model 72 are easily convertible from .22 Long Rifle to .25 automatic, (and vice versa) by simply switching the breech block, barrel and magazine.

The Model 71 is, to some eyes, short, fat and ugly. I can't agree with the last reaction. In these days of modern, streamlined contours, the Plainfield still looks like a gun in the old tradition. It is rather hefty, and there's a reason for this. As originally designed, it was intended to also be made in .380 chambering, and the frame dimensions allow for this. At this time the .380 is still in the works.

There are several good points in the design of the Model 71 aside from its convertibility and easy takedown. The top of the external hammer is deeply but not sharply cross-grooved to give a good thumb-grip for cocking. The trigger is vertically grooved and is unusually wide—it spans the full width of the trigger guard. This gives the same effect as a trigger shoe and offers outstanding control. The magazine release, located at the lower rear of the grip frame, is stirrup-shaped and encloses the entire lower rear corner of the magazine. The magazine has serrations on both sides of the follower guide, allowing it to be pulled downward as the cartridges are loaded. The square-silhouette sights are very heavy and rugged and not susceptible to damage. There are no non-ferrous (al-

The arrow points to the takedown key, the heavy block that retains the breech block in the slide. The factory calls this the "lock" piece."

94

Takedown of the Model 71 is extremely simple. Note the separate breech block.

loy) parts in the gun, very few of stamped steel and only one of molded plastic—the magazine follower.

Though it may seem odd in such a modern pistol, there are flat springs in the design, powering the trigger bar/disconnector and the magazine release. These are U-shaped rather than V-shaped, however, and are not subject to severe flexing. I doubt that they will be prone to breakage. In any event, parts are readily available from the manufacturer. The grips are a nice surprise, in this day of plastics, as they are checkered and grooved walnut. There is one thing about them, though, that may be cause for concern: The grips meet at the rear, forming the backstrap of the pistol, and at lower rear they are unsupported. If the gun were dropped and happened to land on that point, the grips would be badly broken.

My main criticism of the Model 71 is the safety system. Not that it doesn't work properly—in fact, it's a very positive and efficient hammer-block type. Here is the problem: The Model 71 has a full-reach, non-inertia firing pin. When the hammer is fully down, the firing pin point protrudes from the breech face—or, rests against the

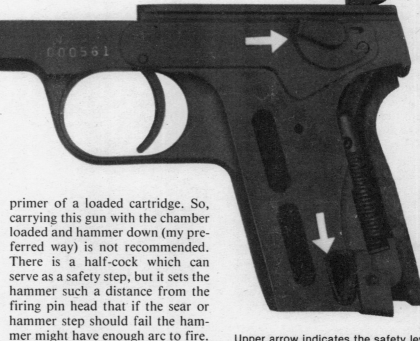

Upper arrow indicates the safety lever which must not be turned beyond its usual arc with grip removed. Lower arrow points to the flat U-shaped magazine catch spring.

primer of a loaded cartridge. So, carrying this gun with the chamber loaded and hammer down (my preferred way) is not recommended. There is a half-cock which can serve as a safety step, but it sets the hammer such a distance from the firing pin head that if the sear or hammer step should fail the hammer might have enough arc to fire. Actually, there are three perfectly safe ways to carry the gun with chamber loaded: with hammer at full-cock and safety applied; with hammer at half-cock and safety on; or with safety on and hammer fully down. The last mentioned requires that the hammer be pulled back before the safety can be released. Two of these methods, though, require two separate operations to get the gun into action. The first, carrying at full-cock,

An extremely wide trigger gives excellent leverage. To avoid damage, it should not be pulled hard while hammer is at half-cock.

means that only the safety must be turned, and here, again, there is a problem. The safety lever has no serrations, only a raised rib and poor leverage. As a personal protection piece, the gun has limitations. As a casual plinker or home protection gun, the added safety factor might be welcome.

Speaking of the safety, removal of the left grip allows it to be turned beyond its normal arc. Don't. When it reaches a certain point, the little positioning ball can depart, never to be seen again. Also, when the hammer is at half-cock, never pull hard on the trigger, as this can break or deform the upper projections of the trigger, or damage the trigger bar/disconnector.

The walnut grips meet at the rear to form the backstrap, and at lower rear they are unsupported and potentially breakable.

P.A.F. "Junior" Pistol

At the time it was made, from 1954 to 1957, this little .25 automatic had the distinction of being the only handgun commercially produced on the African continent. It was designed by a Dutch immigrant, Mr. P. Nagel, and was manufactured by the Pretoria Arms Factory, Limited, of Pretoria, South Africa. The basic design of the gun is of the familiar Browning pattern with a few touches from other sources. The barrel, for example, has a single retaining lug, much like the one in the Czech Model 45 pistol. The disconnector is an upward projection of the trigger bar, like the system used in the 1934 Beretta. There is, in fact, only one truly original touch in the design: When the manual safety is turned upward to the on-safe position, it cams a small pin vertically upwards out of the frame into a recess in the underside of the slide, locking the slide closed. The safety also blocks the sear, of course.

There are several deficiencies in the design of the "Junior" pistol. The pivot points of both the extractor and the sear are badly placed, resulting in poor mechanical advantage. The same can be said of the trigger, its pivot point being at the rear rather than at the top of the trigger. The trigger pull is quite stiff, and the lower edge of the trigger tends to pinch the finger. The magazine is of very thin steel stock, and in one pistol I examined, a split had developed at the top of the back panel.

P.A.F. apparently had some difficulty in maintaining the proper level of heat treatment, as some of the guns I've seen showed signs of being a little "soft." In one case, where the gun had obviously been fired a great deal, there were indications of stress and bending at the front lower projection of the slide and at the striker spring base at the upper rear of the frame.

The rather ornately embossed grips are of black plastic and are retained by two screws on each side. These are located very near the edge of the top forward and lower rear corners, and chipping in those areas is not unusual. As with all of the parts for this scarce little gun, no replacements are available commercially, other than an occasional pistol stripped out by a used-parts dealer.

The "Junior" is very thin and flat, measuring only $\frac{27}{32}$ of an inch at its widest point through the grips. A very few slightly larger prototypes were made in .32 auto chambering, but this caliber was never put into production. After manufacturing of the .25 ceased in 1957, the Pretoria Arms Factory (P.A.F.) was closed down, and these little pistols passed into the realm of the collector. According to official sources in South Africa, only about 2,000 of these guns were made.

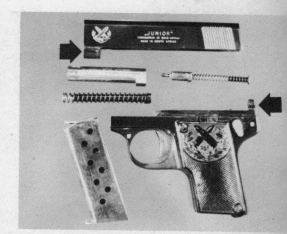

In this field-stripped view of the P.A.F. Junior, the arrows indicate the areas of stress, where prolonged use can cause bending.

Protector Palm Pistol

This odd little gun was originally designed by Jacques Turbiaux of France, and was first offered for sale in 1883. Ten years later the design was improved by an American, P.H. Finnegan. The guns were marketed in the U.S. under the name "Protector," and examples have been seen bearing various company names, such as "Chicago Fire Arms Co." and "Minneapolis Fire-Arms Co."; but, some authorities believe that those made in this country were actually manufactured by the Ames Sword Company of Chicopee Falls, Massachusetts. The original French-made guns, which differ slightly, are marked "Le Protector," and "Systeme Turbiaux."

The pistol has a seven-shot radial "cylinder"—actually, a flat heavy ring with chambers bored around its edge like spokes in a wheel. The pistol is held in the palm of the hand with the barrel protruding between the fingers, and the heel of the hand squeezes a large lever at the rear which rotates the magazine and cocks and drops the internal hammer. On the American models there is a one-finger grip-type safety at the front beside the barrel. Many people, on first picking up one of these guns, will hold it with the free end of the lever pointing downward, but this position makes firing awkward, and the original factory instructions show the gun gripped in the hand with the lever pointing upward. The cartridge, like the gun, is now in the realm of the collector. The cartridge itself was a rimfire type, called the .32 Extra Short. It may be of passing interest to note that this same cartridge was the one used in the Remington-Rider Magazine Pistol, made from 1871 to 1888. This round was discontinued in 1920.

The pistol's four springs are all of the flat blade-type, and breakage is not uncommon. The hammer spring is a crescent-shaped part that is riveted to the inner wall of the magazine well and is rather severely flexed during the firing cycle. The same can be said of the firing lever return spring, an external, curved blade which is screw-mounted on the lever and bears on the outside of the frame. This one would be fairly simple to make, but the hammer spring would be quite a problem. Replacement parts are, of course, virtually impossible to find. The internal magazine rotation spring and grip safety spring are relatively easy to reproduce, although the former does require rather precise fitting.

The Protector Palm Pistol with magazine cover and radial magazine removed. The arrow points to the broken end of the hammer spring which should extend its crescent shape to meet the base of the hammer near the shank of the arrow.

This discussion on putting the gun back in firing order is academic, as no cartridges are available. Collectors, however, prefer to have their pieces working properly, even if they are never to be fired. The circular "grips" are of black molded hard rubber, and it may be that the odd shape of the gun caused it to be accidentally dropped with some frequency. At any rate, these circles of hard rubber are frequently broken. Needless to say, there are no replace-ments. This applies also to the hard rubber "pad" on the back of the firing lever.

Perhaps one of the reasons for the lack of acceptance and eventual disappearance of this design was the fact that when the round being fired was aligned with the barrel, there were two rounds pointing back toward the shooter. When you consider the relative instability of some of the early priming compounds, this may have caused some to be concerned.

Iver Johnson Top-Break Revolver

The old-timers call it the "owl-head," after the well-known trademark found on the grips. In good original condition or properly rebuilt, the old Iver Johnson will make a very dependable home protection gun. Although a .22 version was made, most of those encountered will be in .38 S&W or .32 S&W caliber. Both internal and external hammer types were available.

In its day, one of the main selling points was a safety feature which has since been used on several modern revolvers—a movable bar to transfer the hammer blow to the firing pin. In the Iver Johnson, the "safety lifter" was a hammer lever which had an upper extension that was brought into position between the hammer and firing pin only when the trigger was pulled all the way to the rear. The hammer struck the lifter extension, which struck the firing pin. When the trigger was in forward position, the lifter was down, and the face of the hammer had a recess so it couldn't touch the firing pin head. Early Iver Johnson advertisements showed the external hammer type gun with the revolver hammer being struck by a carpenter's hammer, inviting those who wished to test the safety feature to "hammer

the hammer." It was a good system, and these guns were made for a long while—from 1892 to 1950.

The lifter extension receives a heavy impact from the hammer, but this is somewhat cushioned by the primer of the cartridge. If the gun is snapped a lot while it's empty, though, the repeated sharp impact will eventually cause crystallization and breakage of the lifter. Dry-firing can also cause firing pin breakage and crushing of the firing pin return spring.

Another chronic ailment of these guns is one which is common to most other top-break guns of that era: The frames were mild steel castings, and the T-type barrel latch was mechanically inefficient. They are often found to be loose. There are several ways to correct this, including detail-stripping the frame, adding a spot of steel weld to the back of each latching lug and recutting them to fit. This is the hard way.

If the looseness is not too great, a method I often use is to place a small fitted block tightly between the lugs to prevent bending, rest the lugs alternately on the edge of an anvil, and use a hammer and blunt punch to make an impression on the side of each lug, about midway, near the rear edge. The result

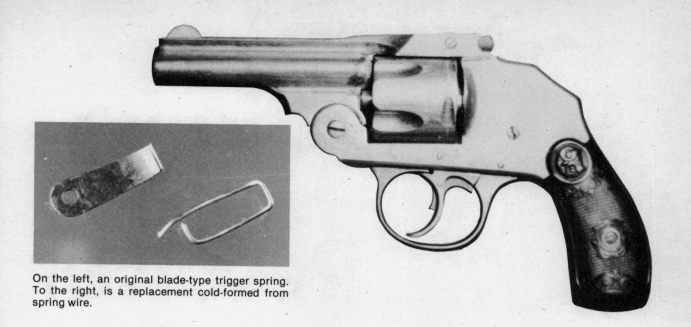

On the left, an original blade-type trigger spring. To the right, is a replacement cold-formed from spring wire.

is a slight bump on the back surface of each lug, and this will tighten the latch. When you do this, use a small hammer, and don't get too close to the edge, or it may chip off. Don't forget the block between the lugs, or they may be bent or broken off.

In later versions of this gun, all springs were of the round-wire type. The older guns used blade- or leaf-type springs throughout, and in most cases this caused no difficulty, but there was one exception—the trigger spring. Instead of the V-type used by most similar guns of this era, the Iver Johnson used a single curved blade with a

hole at one end for the passage of the trigger guard screw. When the trigger is pulled, this spring is flexed rather severely, and it lacks the tension-distribution of the V-type. When it breaks, the amateur, making a new one from pre-tempered stock, will likely burn up a few bits and de-temper the spring in trying to drill the hole. In many cases, he will also over-tighten and strip the guard screw, and this one is not of a common size. There is an easier way. The trigger spring can be made from .037 or .039 piano wire which can be cold-formed. The accompanying photo shows the shape. It must be curved

a little more at the tip than the original leaf-type.

Many parts for these old "IJ" revolvers are still available, both from the factory and from other sources. There are two items that have become increasingly hard to locate—the "safety lifter" and the firing pin cup, or bushing, which screws into the breech face and requires the use of a special two-pronged tool for installation and removal.

I've seen many of these old owl-heads in awful shape, but I've never seen one that couldn't be made to work with a bit of tightening and a new spring or two.

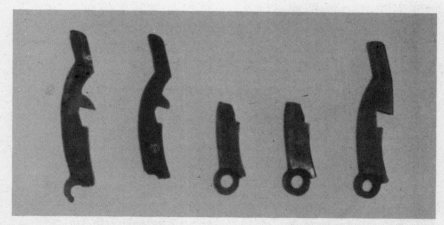

The safety lifter on the far right is intact, those to its left are all broken—replacements are becoming difficult to find.

Clerke First Revolver

A broken original flat hammer spring is at the right. On the left, a doubled round-wire replacement.

It is the custom for many to sneer at the "cheap" handgun. They call them, "Saturday Night Specials," and label them dangerous to the user. They're wrong, of course. Any gun that will fire the one shot that saves its owner from injury or death is a good gun, even if its major parts are of pot-metal and it costs only $20. If some malefactor menaces my family, I can protect the Frau and Kinder with a Walther PPK/S or a Beretta Model 84. But, how about the elderly, and others who are on a small, fixed income? Are they to be denied the right of self protection? Quite often, the availability of "cheap" handguns to the less fortunate law-abiding citizen can mean the difference between life and death. In some neighborhoods, this is no exaggeration—it is an understatement.

The Clerke First model revolver is a cheap handgun. Its major parts are of non-ferrous alloy, and with long and heavy use they will wear quickly and break often. It is, however, a relatively sturdy gun, and with minimum usage, it will serve its purpose and last for many years. If a person buys one of these, takes it out and fires a few rounds for familiarization, cleans it, loads it, and puts it in the bed-side table, it will do the same job as a gun costing much more. The gun is offered in two calibers—.22 rimfire, and .32 Smith & Wesson centerfire.

As with any revolver that has a separate pull-pin release for the cylinder, the most frequent repair I've done on these is replacement of a lost cylinder pin. These are readily available from Clerke Products, 2219 Main Street, Santa Monica, CA 90405. If I happen to be temporarily out of them, it's a simple matter to turn one out. The rod is held in the frame by a small, doubled, round-wire spring which grips a groove on the rod, and these springs will occasionally break or lose tension. Here, again, they are available and also easy to make.

All of the springs in the Clerke are round wire, mostly torsion type, with one exception. The hammer spring is a flat-type, and these break with some frequency, especially after long use. I usually do not replace these with the factory type. A replacement made from doubled, heavy round wire seems to last much longer. At least, I've never had one returned.

A non-gunsmith should never remove the sideplate from a Clerke revolver. When this is done, the

Left arrow points to the trigger spring engagement; the right one indicates the coil cylinder hand spring. Both of these springs are easily detached when the sideplate is removed.

The arrow points to the hammer spring, this one a doubled round-wire replacement.

cylinder hand spring, which fits over a stud on the hand and lies in a recess on the trigger, will often depart with some speed never to be seen again. Also, any movement of the parts with the plate off is likely to detach the trigger spring from the front lip of the trigger, and for the non-professional, replacing it is an interesting endeavor.

The Clerke has thin plastic grips which are stabilized against rotation by two plastic projections which enter wells in the grip frame. Breakage of these is frequent, and on the one shown in the photo,

this has been fixed by installing a pin at the lower edge of the grip frame, drilling a hole in each grip to accept the pin, and facing off the ends of the pin just below the outer surface of the grips.

I know of one instance of main parts breakage in which the rear internal tip of the trigger came off. The gun was much used. Even so, when I sent the broken trigger to the Clerke company, they replaced it right away at no cost to the owner.

It has its limitations. It's a cheap gun. It is not, however, a bad one.

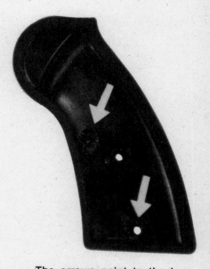

The arrows point to the location of the grip stabilizing studs, which in this example are both broken off. A hole has been drilled at the lower position to match a frame-mounted pin.

The arrow points to the cylinder latch pin, a part that is frequently lost. The one shown is a shop-made replacement.

Raven P-25 Pistol

The past few years have seen the emergence of a large variety of .25 pocket automatics on the American gun market, most of them in the medium to low price range. Prior to the federal law of 1968, many of them were imports. The majority, both U.S.- and foreign-made, were of questionable quality. A very few, even though low priced, were well-made and reliable guns. The Raven P-25, made in Baldwin Park, California, is one of these.

While the basic design is somewhat similar to some of the West German imports, the Raven people seem to have corrected all of the mistakes. Construction is mainly of non-ferrous alloy, but all parts of this material are of sufficient size and strength to avoid any inherent weakness. For example, where some of the imports had a rather fragile open-top slide, the one used on the Raven fully encloses the barrel housing with ample beef at the muzzle end to take the recoil strain.

Another good point is the striker. In most of the true hammerless pistols, this part is a hollow tube with a firing pin point at its forward end and a detent to engage the sear at the lower rear. By its very design, this type is prone to

breakage. In the Raven the sear was placed more forward, and the striker is a solid part with a collar near its forward end to engage the beak of the sear. The rear portion of the striker is inside its spring, which also acts as a guide, and has a slim rearward projection which acts as a cocking indicator. The striker collar will contact the sear at a slightly different point each time, evenly distributing the wear.

Early models of the Raven had a unique safety system—a button-activated sliding plate at the top of the left grip that directly blocked the movement of the sear. With the safety button in the forward on-safe position, drawing back the slide would automatically move the safety into firing position. It was an interesting but impractical feature, and manually moving the safety toward the rear was rather awkward. When I covered the Raven in a magazine article, I commented that a forward off-safe movement might be more convenient, and that the "automatic" movement feature could be eliminated. Perhaps Raven was listening or, more likely, their design engineer came up with the idea on his own. In any event, currently-made Raven pistols have just this arrangement.

The striker spring base, or "retainer" as the factory calls it, is made of alloy but is not under severe stress. No breakage has been seen.

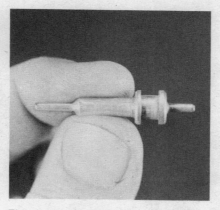

This is the solid striker of the Raven. The firing pin point is at right, indicator pin at left. The "collar" engages the sear.

As mentioned earlier, major parts of the Raven are of alloy, with the barrel and internal operating parts of steel, of course. I have no quarrel with the use of alloy in firearms, as many of these space-age materials have amazing tensile strength. When I originally wrote about the Raven, I questioned the use of alloy in one location—the striker spring base, which the factory calls the "retainer." Although this part is not under great stress, it serves also as the takedown key, and I felt that this part should be made of steel. I have seen many Raven pistols since that time and have fired quite a few rounds through my own, and that little "retainer" has shown absolutely no signs of strain. So, if you read the article, ignore my previous comments.

Since production began, I have repaired exactly one Raven pistol, replacing a striker that had a broken firing pin point. The owner admitted a good deal of snapping with the chamber empty.

Note in the field-stripped view that the striker spring surrounds the tail of the striker—an unusual arrangement.

Remington Model 51 Pistol

Remington's only entry into the field of automatic pistols was designed in 1915 by the famed John D. Pedersen. He spent four years perfecting it, and the pistol was first marketed in the .380 chambering in September, 1919. In 1921 it was also offered in .32 caliber. The pistol was outstanding in two respects. First, Pedersen made considerable effort to produce a grip shape that was the most comfortable for the average hand, and he succeeded. Secondly, the Model 51 is not a true blow-back pistol. It has a separate breech block within the slide which is allowed to recoil about 3/16 of an inch before impinging on an inner shoulder of the slide, producing what might be called a "delayed" or "hesitation" action. One result of this system is a markedly reduced recoil, as felt by the shooter's hand.

There are several notably good features in the Model 51. A wide, matted area extends the full length of the slide top to prevent light reflection, and the sights are as good as those on any modern pistol—square post front, square notch rear. The grip safety acts as a cocking indicator, springing outward only when the hammer is back.

Round-wire helical coil springs were used exclusively in this design

with one exception. In pistols made before 1924 the extractor was a dovetailed type with a tempered tail, acting as its own spring. The design was changed in later guns to an extractor with *no* spring, cammed into operation by the movement of the internal breech block. In case one of the early-type extractors breaks, a used-parts dealer or your gunsmith will be the only recourse, as Remington has no replacement parts.

The separate internal breech block is extensively skeletonized for passage of the firing pin, the extractor recess, and various locking surfaces, and its impinging action deals it a rather sharp blow with each firing. I have seen several cases in which the breech block was cracked, and with the scarcity of parts, the only way to repair this problem is to carefully weld the broken pieces and cut away the excess weld. It's not an easy repair.

Another part that receives considerable stress and occasionally breaks is the barrel lock pin, the key to the takedown of the Model 51. Fortunately, this part is relatively simple to reproduce.

The molded black-rubber grips of the Model 51 are retained in a unique fashion. Double-riveted to

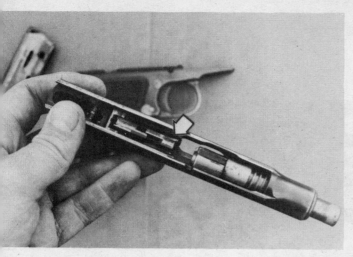

In this view of the dismounted slide, the arrow indicates the separate breech block, here in its forward position.

Arrow points to the barrel lock pin, key to the takedown sequence. Note also large rivet on the grip panel, (one of two)—which hold the internal grip retaining plate.

the inside of each grip is a large thin plate of steel which is keyed under shelves in the grip frame. To remove the grips, the grip safety pin at the lower rear of the grip is drifted in until it's even with the frame, then the grip is slid downward a short distance until it clears the locking shelves and can be lifted off to the side. The process is then repeated with the opposite grip. It is neither necessary (nor advisable!) to remove the grip safety pin from the frame—just drift it back and forth enough to clear the grips. Because of this method of retention, breakage of grips presents a real problem, as making a pair by hand still leaves the question of how they can be attached. Fortunately, the grips are well-supported by the frame and are not often broken.

Production ended in 1927, and one of the best American pocket pistols is now in the realm of the collector. In that area, it might be well to note that a larger version was made experimentally in .45 caliber, and that in the pocket version, more were produced in .380 than in .32 chambering.

The Model 51, field-stripped. Arrow at upper left points to the springless extractor. Right arrow indicates the separate breech block. At lower left, arrow points to the barrel lock pin.

Ruger Standard Model Automatic

In 1949, William Ruger and the late Alex Sturm began production of an automatic pistol for the .22 Long Rifle cartridge, a pistol so well-designed that it has remained essentially unchanged during its entire period of production. Just as the name Ruger is similar to Luger, the gun shares with the famed German pistol its general shape and inherently good pointing qualities.

Internally, however, the Ruger is entirely different. By employing a cylindrical bolt and a tubular receiver well-mated to a stamped and welded frame, the design avoids much complicated machining. This, along with other manufacturing innovations, has helped to keep the price moderate in spite of rising production costs. It is, how-

ever, in no way a cheap pistol where quality is concerned. Fit and finish, materials and workmanship are comparable to pistols costing considerably more.

During its inception, Ruger must have concentrated on perfecting the feed and ejection systems. The rimmed, lead-bullet .22 Long Rifle cartridge is all wrong for a semi-automatic, but the Ruger is notable for its freedom from jamming. In fact, I remember examining one Ruger in which the extractor was missing entirely, and it was jamming only occasionally! This is a vivid testimonial to the efficiency of the pistol's feed and ejection system. The magazine is of particularly sturdy construction, and throughout the pistol round-wire springs are used exclusively. Only the trigger, magazine follower and magazine endpiece are of alloy, everything else being of steel except the grip panels.

So much careful thought went into the Ruger design that I can think of only one quirk: The safety button, located just to the rear of the left grip top, is attached to its internal plate by riveting. The button contains a side-mounted, spring-loaded ball which bears on notches in the frame to hold the safety in its two positions. In sev-

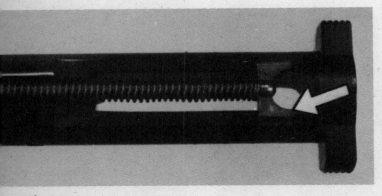

The arrow points to one of the two wings of the recoil spring guide where breakage occasionally occurs.

back against the housing. This will insure that the lower end of the strut makes proper contact with the mainspring plunger. This point is particularly important since the pistol can be assembled with the strut swung forward, out of contact with the follower. If this is the case, it will immediately be obvious, as the bolt cannot be fully retracted.

The "wings" at the rear end of the recoil spring assembly have been known to break, but I have seen several guns in which one wing was completely missing, and there was no malfunction. The problem was discovered only when the pistols were taken down for cleaning or refinishing. The last time I checked the price, this entire assembly cost only around $2, and does not require a gunsmith for installation, so it's not a major fault. All parts are, of course, available from the factory.

On some of the early guns, the ball detent in the safety button (arrow) loosens, allowing it to rotate and malfunction. It's an easy repair.

eral pistols I have examined over the years, the riveting had loosened, allowing the button to rotate and putting the safety out of commission. It should be noted that in all cases the pistols were of early manufacture, and I have seen no recent instances of this, so it's likely that the problem has already been corrected by more positive riveting at the factory. Anyhow, the problem is simple to repair. Just be sure that the button is properly positioned in the plate before re-riveting.

The only other problem that occurs involves reassembly. When preparing to swing the mainspring housing back into the grip frame, be sure the hammer is in the down (fired) position. With the pistol inverted, tilt the barrel slightly upward until the hammer strut falls

Savage Model 1908 Pocket Automatic

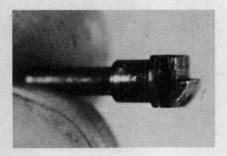

The arrow points to the location of the Savage 1908's sear-trip catch which can be potentially troublesome. In the close-up shot below you will see the "beak" of the sear-trip catch. If it breaks, the pistol may fire fully auto.

When the Savage Company first produced a pistol from E. H. Searle's patents of 1905, it was chambered for the .45 automatic cartridge and was entered in the U.S. Ordnance tests of 1907. When it was not accepted, the design was scaled down to .32 caliber and marketed as the Savage Model 1908. It was later offered in .380 chambering, and in 1917 the pistol was slightly redesigned. At one point, experimentally, a very few pistols were made in .25 caliber. Today, the one most frequently encountered is the .32 caliber Model 1908.

One of the main points of the design is the turning barrel locking system. Controlled by a stud on top of the barrel and a track inside the slide, the barrel must rotate slightly to free the slide for rearward travel. The twist of the rifling is opposite to the direction of this movement, and the interaction of bullet and rifling tends to oppose the barrel rotation. Considering the very small degree of rotation, the Savage pistols are actually semi-locked, or retarded blowback automatics. For the .32 and .380 cartridges, the system is really unnecessary, but it works perfectly and may add a few feet-per-second to the velocity of the bullet.

Another notable feature of the Savage pistols is the use of a double-column or stagger-type magazine, holding 10 rounds in .32, nine in .380. This pistol was also one of the first to use an around-the-barrel recoil spring, allowing a low barrel position which aids both feeding and accuracy.

The main trouble area in these pistols is in the disconnector system. The sear and striker are both located in the breech block which travels with the slide. The trigger bar, which contacts and trips the sear when the trigger is pressed, is pushed down by the recoiling slide and caught and held in the frame by a small spring-powered detent. Some parts lists refer to this as the "sear-trip catch." If it breaks, the pistol will still operate, but with one important difference: When the trigger is pulled, it will empty the magazine, full-auto!

Another source of difficulty is the original grip material—hard rubber. The grips slide into upper and lower dovetails from the rear and are retained by projections on the back which drop into wells in the frame. Hard rubber has some flexibility but lacks impact resistance, and the Savage grips are

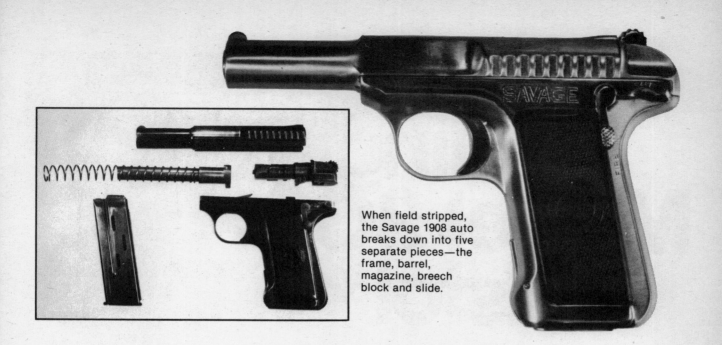

When field stripped, the Savage 1908 auto breaks down into five separate pieces—the frame, barrel, magazine, breech block and slide.

centrally unsupported. Unbroken original grips are a rare sight. Plastic modern reproductions are available, and if obtained in black color, are very much like the originals in appearance.

For reasons of safety, I should point out one odd feature of these pistols: The part at the top rear of the slide is *not* a hammer. It is a lever which cocks the striker (firing pin) during recoil and is directly connected to the striker. When the cocking lever is in the "down" position, the striker is all the way forward with the firing pin point protruding through the breech face. If a round is in the chamber, the firing pin point will be resting

on the primer, a most unhealthy situation, especially if the pistol were dropped or otherwise jarred. There is no provision for a safety-step or half-cock. So, the only safe way to carry the Savage with a round in the chamber is with the striker cocked and manual safety applied. Personally, I prefer to treat it as a "hammerless" pistol, filling its large-capacity magazine and leaving the chamber empty until just before firing is intended.

Repair parts will be a problem, as Savage ran out of these years ago. Certain original parts can sometimes be obtained from the used-parts dealers. If this proves to be impossible, most internal parts, such as the sear-trip catch, can be made by any competent gunsmith. The Savage pistols are definitely worth repairing, as they are made of good materials, and basically it's an excellent design.

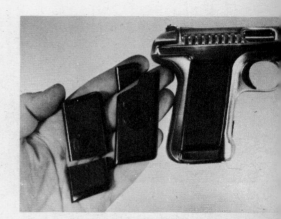

The original hard-rubber grips are subject to frequent breakage. Fortunately, modern plastic replacements are available.

Separate breech block with the striker in the fired position. There is no half-cock provision so, if you want to carry the Savage with a round in the chamber, the striker must be cocked with the manual safety applied.

Sterling Model 302 Pistol

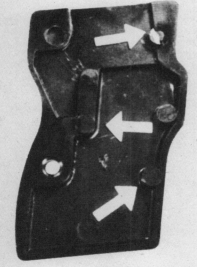

Plastic grip panels are stabilized against rotation by several small studs on their inside surfaces. These tend to break off, as has the one by the tail of the middle arrow.

One of the very few American pocket pistols chambered for the .22 Long Rifle cartridge, this gun has an almost identical counterpart—the Sterling Model 300 in the .25 auto chambering. The .22 version, the Model 302, made its debut in May of 1973. With some small manufacuturing modifications, it is very similar to the Italian Rigarmi pistol, made by Rino Galesi, not to be confused with the Armi Galesi guns. Both were imported into the U.S. in considerable quantity prior to 1968. The Sterling is in some respects a sturdier gun, generally less prone to breakage than its Italian brother. The Rigarmi guns were not as well-made as those of Armi Galesi.

As in any striker-fired automatic, especially one of .22 rimfire chambering, the firing system of the Sterling is susceptible to breakage, particularly from dry-firing, snapping the gun on an empty chamber. A metallurgist has told me that breakage of this type is due to something called "impact drift," in which the firing pin, stopped sharply by striking the inside of its tunnel in the slide, becomes more brittle in its forward extremity because of increasing density of the steel. Translated into everyday language, this means that if you keep snapping it empty, the firing pin point will get as hard as glass, and eventually snap off. In actual firing, the point strikes the soft brass of the case, and its stop is, by comparison, cushioned.

When the striker point breaks in the Sterling, repair in the shop, that is, repointing, will not be feasible. The point is offset from center in the .22, being right at the edge of the striker body. Fortunately, replacement parts are readily available at most gunsmiths and from the manufacturer.

Another point of occasional difficulty is the ejector, which is a slim projection from the forward end of the striker spring guide. As the slide recoils, this projection emerges through a hole in the center of the striker and a corresponding hole in the breech face to kick out the fired case. If this ejector pin is bent out of line, or breaks away from the guide, it can deform the striker spring and cause a serious jam. In one gun I examined, the broken ejector pin lodged in such a way that the recoil imparted enough force to bend the striker spring base. It should be pointed out that this is not a common occurrence, and the one mentioned above was a very early pis-

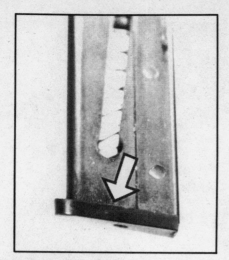

Made from plastic, the magazine floorplate can be broken if the magazine is dropped.

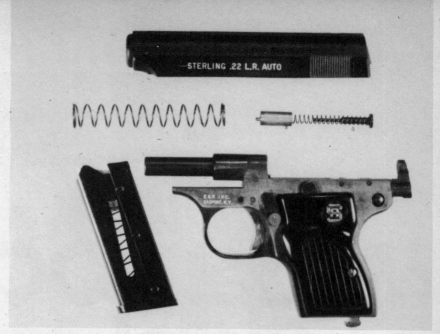

Takedown of the Sterling 302 is relatively simple and straight forward.

tol, perhaps having an error in the heat treatment of the ejector/ guide. It would be well, though, to occasionally examine this part in your gun, and if it appears out of line, replace it.

The original grips are made of a good-quality modern plastic and retained by one screw on each side. They are stabilized against rotation by several protrusions on the inside which bear against the side openings in the frame. These little plastic positioning studs shear off with some regularity, and several shooters I know, who like and use the Sterling, have given up after the third set of grips, and made their own from walnut, carefully inletting them to fit the openings.

The magazine of the Model 302 is of particularly good design, a very strong one with separate front and rear sections electrically welded at three points on each side. The front section enters the rear part and stops short of the rear wall, its inner edges forming a rim guide for the cartridges. The guide slots for the follower button are angled to slightly change the tilt of the alloy follower as each round is fed, keeping the delivery angle constant. If a Sterling misfeeds, it's because some accident has deformed the magazine, not

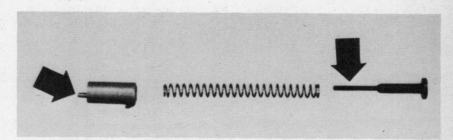

The offset firing pin point (left arrow) is susceptible to breakage, especially from dry-firing. The ejector (right arrow) is integral with the striker spring guide and, if bent or broken, can cause serious trouble.

because of the Sterling design.

With the exception of the alloy magazine follower, the Model 302 has only one other non-steel part— the floorplate of the magazine. This is made of plastic, and as magazines are often subject to fumbling by chilled hands and being dropped on hard surfaces, I've had to replace several of these which were broken. For one shooter, I replaced his broken floorplate with one of formed sheet steel with a projection at lower rear to take up the difference in thickness and meet the magazine catch.

The safety lever is conveniently located and positively blocks the trigger, but with all true hammerless pistols I recommend carrying them with the chamber empty, cycling the slide just before firing

is intended. On some of the early pistols, I found it necessary to relieve the inside of the extractor, to allow slightly more inward reach for the extractor beak, as fired cases were being dropped before they were struck by the ejector. The factory has apparently ironed this out, as I haven't encountered it lately.

There is one other point that should be remembered, as it is shared with many other small .22 pistols. The Model 302 may prove to be more reliable with certain brands of ammunition than with others. Try several, and when you find the brand that works best, stay with it. It's a good, solid little gun and has recently become available in stainless steel.

Sterling Model 400 Pistol

Unlike the smaller Sterling pistols, the .380 Model 400 is an entirely new design. Its size and weight take it out of the pocket pistol class and make it a medium automatic —a holster gun. With its double-action trigger system and external hammer, it can serve well as a police back-up gun or a pistol for home and personal defense. Another good point is its price. For a pistol in this caliber having the same general features, the cost can be almost double the modest tag of the Sterling. The Model 400 is well-made of good materials, and its size and comfortable grip make it pleasant to shoot, even with the new warmer .380 loads.

The takedown system of the Model 400 is very simple, and there is no operational difficulty or potential for breakage. It consists of a pivoting block of steel on the frame, just forward of the trigger pin, which is controlled by a spring-locked, screw-slotted button. With a screwdriver of suitable size, the button is pushed inward, then turned clockwise toward the muzzle to swing the block downward. This allows the slide to be pulled back beyond its usual limit, lifted up at the rear, and run forward off the frame. While the takedown block is spring-locked when in the non-takedown position, there is no provision for its automatic return to that position. This must be done manually during reassembly. In other words, it would be quite possible to put the slide back on the gun, leave the block in the lowered takedown position, and fire the pistol in this condition! It is doubtful that this would cause any injury to the shooter, but it could result in a spectacular jam and possible deformation of some internal parts. The main point here is that the shooter should be thoroughly familiar with this takedown system. As a general rule, when the screw-slotted head of the take-

The magazine catch (arrow) is a heavy blade-type spring, screw-mounted on the frame inside the right grip panel. It is not flexed enough to be broken during normal operation.

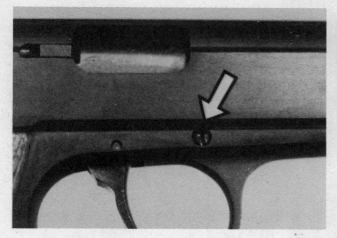

In this view, the inner takedown block is in the unlocked position, ready for slide removal—its slotted head is recessed below the frame surface (arrow). Unfortunately, the gun can be fired in this condition.

The arrow indicates the screw-like head of the takedown lever, here shown locked in its proper position, even with the surface of the frame.

down button is about level with the frame surface, it is properly locked. When it is recessed below the frame surface, it is probably in the takedown position. If your gun is new, and you have the instruction booklet, follow the ancient adage: When all else fails, read the instructions.

The push-button style magazine release of the Model 400 is of unusual design. The actual catch is a heavy blade-type spring, screw-mounted on the frame inside the right grip panel. Although flat springs are usually more susceptible to breakage, this one is not subjected to severe flexing and should not break in normal use.

On the Model 400 the only part I have actually replaced is the combination ejector and slide latch, or hold-open device. This part is of stamped, formed sheet steel, and in steel of this weight the proper heat treatment can sometimes be difficult. I think this may have been the problem in both of the cases I examined, as the part was drawn very hard. It receives frequent impact toward the rear from the head of each fired case and a rough jolt from the opposite direction as it stops the slide open when the last round is fired. In both cases, the part had snapped at its

narrowest point—the elbow just below its forward-mounted pivot. I would hasten to add that the factory replaced the part on both guns at no charge, and if this proves to be a chronic ailment, they will likely watch their heat treatment more closely.

The spring that keeps this part in lowered position when it is not performing its hold-open function is formed of flat stock, but this one, also, is not under great tension in normal operation. If one of these should break, they are readily available from Sterling and would likely be replaced under the company's unusually liberal guarantee.

The safety catch of the Model

400 is of the general Walther pattern, shielding the firing pin head from the hammer. Happily, though, it does not automatically drop the hammer when applied. The shielding appears to be of ample depth, so that it would be effective even in the case of slight play in the pivot drum. On a true double-action pistol of this type, I feel that a manual safety is largely unnecessary, but it's there, and it works.

Though the grips appear to be made of wood, they're actually a tough plastic-composition material, well-supported by the frame. I doubt that they will break easily.

The return spring for the combination ejector and slide latch is of formed flat stock but seldom breaks. The ejector/slide latch, however, has been known to snap at its forward narrowed section.

H&R Self-loading Pistol

The Harrington & Richardson Self-loading pistol in .32 caliber shows its obvious Webley ancestry.

Like Colt and Smith & Wesson, Harrington & Richardson went abroad for their first pocket automatic design. The original patents were taken out by W. J. Whiting, design engineer for Webley & Scott, Ltd., of Birmingham, England, and made by Webley as the Model 1906. This version had an external hammer, among other differences, and came to be called the Metropolitan Police model. Mr. Whiting came to America in 1905, seeking to license the patent rights, and successfully interested H&R in the undertaking. The design was modified to a striker-fired true hammerless pistol, and U.S. patents were issued in 1907 and 1909. In 1912, the pistol was made by H&R in .25 caliber, and the .32 came along in 1916, continuing in production until 1939.

To those accustomed to Browning-pattern pistols, its external appearance may seem a bit strange, but this is one of the very good ones. It has a comfortable grip with space for all of the fingers and points well. All of the mechanical parts are rugged, and breakage is very unusual. The extractor has a pin on its top which protrudes when the chamber is loaded, one of the first uses of a cartridge indicator. The magazine release is

pure Webley—a button at the lower rear of the grip frame that is pushed straight inward. The grip safety blocks the sear, and the manual safety lever completely disconnects the trigger bar engagement. The ejection port is very large, the magazine is well-made, and these guns rarely malfunction. The takedown is simple and results in only three components, including the magazine, with all springs remaining captive. Finally, there are no flat springs in the design, unless you count the trigger guard, a heavy part which is tempered to serve as the takedown key, locking the barrel in place. I have never seen one of these broken.

As always, there are a few minus points in the design. The grips are of molded hard rubber, and one area is particularly fragile. Just forward of the safety lever on the left side is a narrow projection which seems to be broken off on two out of three pistols examined. This tip is easily broken in careless grip removal, so there is some question whether this breakage has occurred in normal use and operation. Unfortunately, this is not one

A field-stripped H&R pistol, showing its outstanding simplicity. Note the small projections at the top forward edge of the left grip, where breakage may occur.

of the grips that have been commercially reproduced, so any replacements would have to be hand-made.

The manual safety lever moves in an odd direction, the on-safe position being back and down. To go into firing position, the movement is up and forward, a rather unhandy operation. Early models of this gun had a magazine safety, making it impossible to fire with the magazine removed, and this was one of the first uses of this device. In later production, the feature was dropped, so the gun you encounter may or may not have it.

As with any striker-type pistol, excessive snapping when empty will tend to crystallize the firing pin point. No parts are available, but repointing of this part is not difficult for any competent gunsmith. There is a flanged sliding plate at the rear of the slide which retains the striker, recoil block and their attendant springs and guides, and I strongly advise against removal by the amateur. When the non-gunsmith slides this plate off, things will happen faster than the eye can follow, unless, by ill chance, the eye happens to be in the way—remember the safety glasses.

I view the H&R as a definite improvement on Whiting's original design, a combination of old-world skill and American innovation. It is a strong and simple pistol, and it's a pity that only around 40,000 of them were made in the .32 chambering, as the collectors have taken it out of the realm of the shooter. The .25 is somewhat scarcer, incidentally—only about 20,000 of those were made.

H&R Top-Break Revolver

This is the trigger, cylinder hand, and hammer lever assembly. Note the flat spring mounted in front of the hand, giving tension to both hand and lever.

Introduced in 1878, this was the first H&R revolver to have a double-action firing system and automatic ejection of cartridges when opened. The latter feature is reflected in the factory designation, as they called it the "Auto Ejecting" model. It was made in two calibers, a five-shot .38 and a six-shot .32, both cartridges being the standard S&W centerfire rounds.

During its time of production, there were a few small modifications in the design. Very early guns have a blade-type spring for the barrel latch, retained inside the barrel extension by a short screw. Not only do these break often, but removal of the screw for replace-ment requires an angle-point screwdriver and several words not used in polite company. I always replace this spring with one of modified design in round wire.

Most early guns will also have an ejector cam-trip with an external button which allows the automatic feature to be overridden—useful when the gun is being opened just to check the load, rather than to eject fired cases.

The neck of this cam-trip but-ton, near the point where it con-tacts the beak of the ejector cam, is very narrow, and the forward end of the button is somewhat pointed, making it susceptible to catching on clothing. These break often, taking the ejector out of operation, and their odd shape makes repro-duction difficult. The only parts available are those occasionally found in the stock of the used-parts dealers.

Another troublesome thing, found on the early guns, is the cylinder retaining system. This consists of a flat, irregularly-shaped little part with a lower beak that contacts the rear edge of the cylinder and a forward nose held by a spring-powered push-button, located on the left side of the bar-rel extension. The retainer breaks at its pivot point, and the very

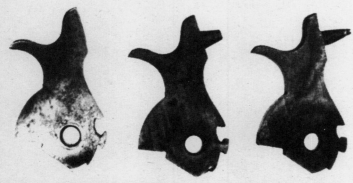

The firing pin is integral with the hammer, and breakage is not un-usual. The one at the extreme right is unbroken.

(Left) The molded hard-rubber grips are rather fragile. The one at left is, for the time being, intact.

(Above) This Harrington & Richardson top-break revolver is a late model five-shot in .38 caliber. This gun was also made in a six-shot .32 version.

short spring which powers the release often collapses, allowing the cylinder to climb out when the gun is opened. I have made exact replacements for the cylinder retainer, but it's not my preferred way to spend the afternoon. More often, I bypass the entire system and drill a tiny hole in the underside of the barrel extension for a very small pin with just enough protrusion to bear on the rear edge of the cylinder.

On the early guns the hammer, trigger and sear are all powered by flat springs with a fairly high rate of breakage. Replacements of original type are available from several sources, and these require a small amount of fitting. Or, they can be replaced with round-wire types of slightly different shape. The cylinder hand and hammer lever are also powered by a flat spring, mounted on the front of the hand. This one is not difficult to make, but proper fitting and shaping usually requires the services of a gunsmith.

The firing pin is an integral part of the hammer and is very susceptible to breakage from extensive dry-firing. The lower front lobe of the hammer, which lifts the hammer lever to draw back the trigger during single-action cocking, also

breaks occasionally. In both cases, it is possible to drill the hammer and install steel pins to perform these functions.

The original grips are of molded hard rubber and seem to be even more fragile than most of this type. And now, the good news: This is one of the grips that has been commercially reproduced, and the modern plastic replacements will last a lot longer than the originals.

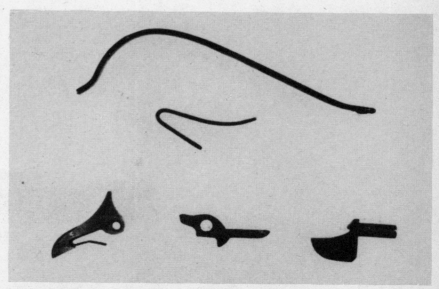

At the top is the blade-type hammer spring, and beneath it the flat V-shaped trigger spring, both of which break with some frequency. Lower, left to right: The sear, with its V-blade spring, the cylinder retainer, and the ejector cam-trip.

H&R Model 922 Revolver

For many years, the long, slim barrel and ham-shaped handle of the H&R Model 922 revolver was a familiar sight in the packs of campers and trappers and in the fishermen's tackle boxes. Before the days of the cast alloy frame, it was the answer for the shooter who was looking for an economical, dependable .22 revolver. Over the years, the 922 has had several design changes, but there are still large numbers of the original model in use.

This is a solid-frame revolver with a spring latch on the front of the frame to release the cylinder pin. Taking out the pin allows the cylinder to drop out for loading, and the pin itself can be used to push out any cases that don't fall free. It's a simple system and works perfectly, but there are a couple of things that can happen if you're careless. The slim cylinder pin can easily be dropped (disappearing in the tall grass), and until you can get a new one, the gun is out of commission. Also, the cylinder ratchet is integral with the body of the cylinder. If the cylinder is dropped, and there is damage to the precisely cut steps of the ratchet, it's possible that the entire cylinder may have to be replaced.

In an unusual arrangement, the

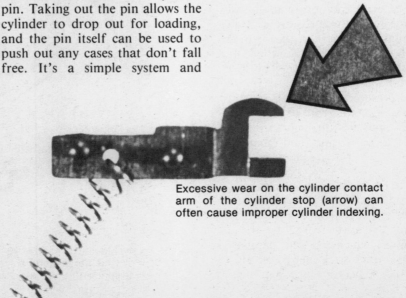

Excessive wear on the cylinder contact arm of the cylinder stop (arrow) can often cause improper cylinder indexing.

The arrow points to the cylinder ratchet, an integral part of the cylinder which, if damaged, could require the replacement of the entire cylinder.

cylinder hand is mounted on the hammer lifter, and the lifter is attached to the rear of the trigger. A single spring, stake-mounted on the front of the hand, operates both parts. This small-diameter spring rests in a tiny hole in the top of the trigger. It's weird, but it works. When the spring breaks, though, it's necessary to replace the entire hand and spring unit, as the spring is staked into a small aperture in the hand.

The cylinder stop, the part which locks the cylinder in place for firing, is powered by a light coil spring which extends into the forward base of the trigger guard. The tension of this spring and the engagement of the stop with the front of the trigger have a delicate balance, and adjustment of this system is a job for a competent gunsmith. If the stop is worn where it contacts the slots in the cylinder, it is sometimes possible to heat and bend the top portion of the stop upward to restore proper contact. Here, again, consult your gunsmith.

Some parts for the Model 922 are still available from Harrington & Richardson. Those that they might not have are usually to be found at one of the used-parts dealers. The Model 922 is a good, dependable old gun, and I know of several that have been in continuous use for more than 30 years.

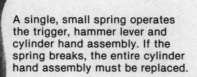

A single, small spring operates the trigger, hammer lever and cylinder hand assembly. If the spring breaks, the entire cylinder hand assembly must be replaced.

Browning Challenger II Pistol

The original Browning Challenger pistol, along with its companion models, the Nomad and the Medalist, came along in 1962. By 1974, it become obvious that these finely-made Belgian .22 pistols could not continue to maintain a reasonable price, due to the drastic rise in both production and importation costs. So, unfortunately, they were phased out of production late in 1974, and for two years there was no .22 pistol in the Browning line. Then, early in 1976, the Browning people announced a new gun, named the Challenger II, entirely made in America. It is a slight redesign of the original Challenger and is in some ways better, I think.

Over the past few years, the only actual repair I've done to a Challenger II was to replace a broken firing pin, and this is the sort of thing that could happen to any gun. From a troubleshooting standpoint, I can only point out areas which might possibly cause some future difficulty, and most of these only apply when the gun is taken apart for cleaning. During replacement of the slide on the receiver, for example, it is necessary to steady the recoil spring and its guide with a forceps or some other tool, or it will kink and be damaged as the slide is pushed back into position.

Removal of the right grip ex-

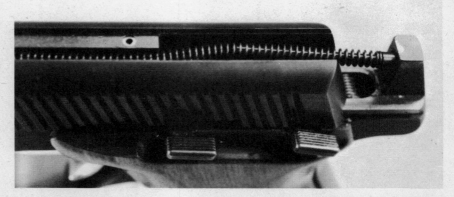

During reassembly, care must be taken that the recoil spring does not kink. Note how the one shown, unsupported, has begun to go out of alignment.

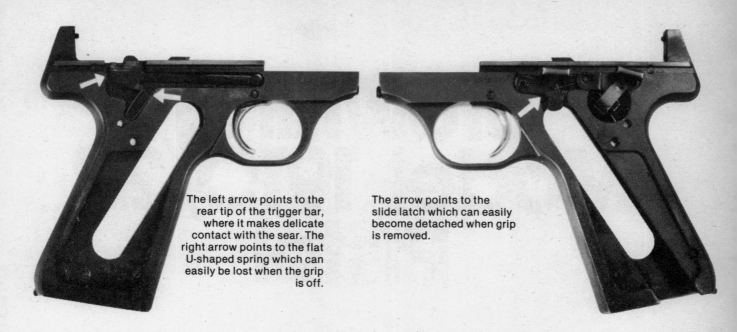

The left arrow points to the rear tip of the trigger bar, where it makes delicate contact with the sear. The right arrow points to the flat U-shaped spring which can easily be lost when the grip is off.

The arrow points to the slide latch which can easily become detached when grip is removed.

poses the combination trigger bar and disconnector, as well as the spring which powers this unit. This spring is a flat U-shaped type and is not severely flexed during normal operation. At the rear tip of the trigger bar, its engagement with the sear is of fairly delicate construction, and extreme pressure on the trigger with the safety locked might possibly cause breakage at this point. For a simple prevention of this, don't pull hard on the trigger with the safety engaged.

Taking off the left grip gives access to the slide latch and manual safety lever, and although these parts are of formed sheet steel, they are well-made and strong. The safety positioning spring is also a blade-type, but here again, it is not extensively flexed and is not likely to break in normal use. Except for the safety, the parts under both grips are retained by the grip panels, so when the grips are removed, one should take care that nothing is lost. This applies especially to the trigger bar spring. If the trigger bar is disturbed while the grip is off, this little piece of U-shaped steel can easily go sproinging away and would be almost impossible to find in a shag rug. On the opposite side, the slide latch is

powered by a round-wire, torsion-type spring, but this one is locked in place around a pin and is in no danger of loss unless other parts are removed.

There is one odd feature of the Challenger II that is not a trouble spot but requires some care in operation. The magazine latch, when the magazine is removed, can swing forward into the magazine entry beyond its latching point and must be pushed back as the magazine is inserted. If this is not done with care, the top cartridge in the magazine may be slightly displaced, and this can cause misfeeding of the first round. The magazine catch needs some sort of limit pin to stop its travel just at the latching point. Perhaps by the time you read this, the Browning people will have done something about this. If not, or if you have an early production gun, just take care when putting in a loaded magazine that the catch is pushed back by the spine of the magazine and not by the top round.

Browning Model 1910/22 Pistol

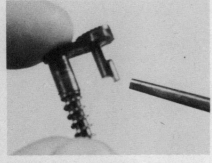

In this photo the tool points to the projection on the safety lever that blocks the movement of the grip safety. The tip is only ⅟₁₆-inch thick. If the safety is in the "on" position and the grip safety is squeezed hard, the tip can snap off.

John M. Browning's patents on this gun cover a wide time span—from 1905 to 1925. The initial shorter version was first offered in 1910, in 7.65mm (.32 auto) only. The 9mm Short (.380 auto) version was not made until 12 years later, in 1922. In the same year, Fabrique Nationale decided to also offer an altered version in both calibers with an eye toward military contract sales. This pistol, designated Model 1922, had a longer barrel and slide, and a longer grip frame and magazine, increasing both the sight radius and magazine capacity. The Model 1922 was adopted as military standard by the Netherlands in 1925 and was also used to some extent by Yugoslavia. Except for the differences noted above, the Model 1922 is exactly the same as the Model 1910 in its internal mechanism.

Even the best designs have their weak points, and this Browning is no exception. The Model 1922 is a true hammerless, striker-fired design, and the safety is more important than in an external-hammer type. There is a grip safety which directly blocks the sear, but this, of course, is pushed in as the pistol is gripped in the hand. The manual side safety, which also acts as a slide lock and takedown aid, is located just to the rear of the left grip top. It does not act directly on the sear, but blocks the grip safety movement. The projection from the safety lever which effects this blockage ends in a bearing point less than ⅟₁₆ of an inch in thickness. A very strong squeeze, or impact on the grip safety with the side safety in "safe" position, can snap off this tiny tip. Also, the only provision for holding the safety lever in "on" or "off" position is a coil spring surrounding the safety pivot shaft and a small shoulder on the lever which requires that the lever be pressed slightly inward while swinging it upward. This arrangement is not sufficient to insure positioning. Brushing against clothing is often enough to push the lever to firing position.

Another design point that is occasionally troublesome is the striker spring base that rises from the rear of the frame. This part rarely breaks off but is prone to bending, and if deformed sufficiently, it will jam the slide. In fairness, it should be pointed out that damage to the spring base is often the result of installation by the amateur gunsmith of a striker spring guide that is too long for the space left when the slide is in full recoil position. A bent spring base

This particular Model 1922 Browning is one of early Nazi Occupation manufacture. The original Model 1910 is almost identical but with a shorter slide, barrel and grip frame.

can often be straightened, but this is a job for the professional gunsmith.

The magazine release, grip safety, sear and trigger bar/disconnector are all powered by a single multi-purpose blade-type spring. In none of these functions, however, is it flexed severely, and breakage is rare. The Model 1910/22 has no more incidence of striker (firing pin) failure than other pistols of similar design, but when one is broken, it may be useful to know that its striker is practically identical with the one used in the early Colt and FN .25 automatics and several others.

In actual use, with the safety limitations in mind, it's best to carry or keep this gun with magazine loaded and chamber empty, operating the slide only when immediate firing is intended. This is a good rule to follow with all hammerless or internal-hammer pistols, no matter how efficient their safety systems.

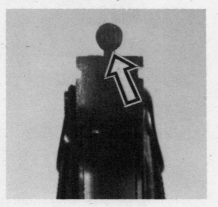

The striker spring base (arrow) rarely breaks; however, it is susceptible to bending if nonoriginal parts are installed in the striker system.

The sear and trigger bar (top arrow) and the magazine catch (bottom arrow) are powered by opposing ends of the same flat spring. It is not severely flexed in normal operation and rarely breaks.

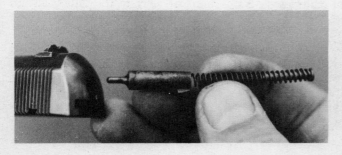

When installing a new striker spring guide, be sure it is original or of standard overall length. One that is too long can bend or break the spring base on the frame.

Browning Hi-Power Pistol

This is the Browning P-35 pistol, also known as the Hi-Power. The one shown was made during the Nazi occupation of Belgium.

In 1926, firearms genius John Moses Browning submitted a patent application for a new pistol, a gun intended to be the final version of the locked-breech system he had originated more than 25 years earlier. The patent was granted in February of 1927, but the designer never knew of it. He died in December, 1926. During the eight years that followed, a succession of prototypes were made at the Fabrique Nationale in Belgium, and finally in 1935 the Hi-Power was born. This name, by the way, has nothing to do with the energy or velocity delivered by the pistol but is a reference to its original 13-round magazine capacity. While we call it the HP, it is known in Europe as the Browning GP, the initials standing for Grande Puissance. It is also frequently called the P-35, after the year of its birth.

The gun was immediately adopted as military standard by Belgium, and several contract orders were filled before WW II interfered. Today, a list of the nations using the Hi-Power as a standard side arm would take up more space than we have here. In addition to the various contract orders, with their special crests and other markings, there have been several major variations of the gun, such as the

ones manufactured in Canada by the John Inglis Company for the Canadian Army and the Republic of China. Some models have a tangent-type adjustable rear sight, others have this sight and a slot for a shoulder-stock/holster. After the war, the pistol in its commercial version was slightly redesigned with changes in the extractor, sear-lever pivot, and other small points. The gun we are considering here is the original model.

This design was so carefully thought out, so precisely engineered, that it's difficult to find any points for real criticism. Except for routine replacement of an occasional broken firing pin, I think I've repaired only three or four of these pistols in the past 30 years. I have observed some cases of weak trigger springs. This is a round-wire torsion type and powers not only the trigger but also the trigger lever that contacts the sear lever in the slide. During disassembly or reassembly, it is easy for the amateur to deform this spring, and this may have been the cause of the weakness. Parts are readily available, and replacement is not difficult.

There are two flat springs in the design. The extractor is tempered to be its own spring, but this is a

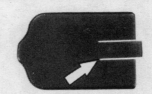

The sear spring (top) is made of formed flat stock, but it is heavy and barely flexed in normal use. Original magazine floorplates have a tempered center section for a retaining latch and may crack at the point shown by the arrow.

Arrow points to the sear-lever retainer, a part sometimes damaged during amateur disassembly. In postwar models, this was changed to a simple cross-pin.

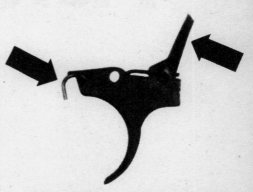

A round-wire trigger spring (left arrow) also powers the trigger lever (right arrow). Occasional weakness of this spring will be encountered.

heavy and sturdy part, and I've never known one to break. The sear spring is a large, flat blade with its lower portion covering the inside rear of the magazine well. The extension at its top which powers the sear is barely flexed in normal operation, and there is no reason to expect breakage.

Current production guns use the hole and lockplate system to retain the magazine floorplate, but originally the rear of the floorplate was double-slotted to free a center piece that was tempered to become a retaining latch. In some cases, especially if the magazine has been frequently disassembled, cracks can develop at the base of the latch strip.

On the original guns, there is a rectangular plate with two inward projections at the center of the retracting serrations on the right side of the slide. One of the inside projections is the pivot for the sear lever, and the other has a semi-circular cut to fit the body of the extractor, retaining the unit in the slide. When the firing pin retainer, firing pin, and extractor are taken out, the sear-lever pivot can easily be removed. I have seen one or two cases in which someone has attempted to drive or pry it out with the other parts in place, doing ex-

tensive damage to the slide. In the postwar models, this part was changed to a simple cross-pin, and the extractor changed to an external pivoting type with a coil spring.

Original grips are of walnut, secured by a single screw on each side and well-supported by the frame. All sorts of custom replacements are available. Most HP pistols will have a magazine safety located inside the trigger, and this can easily be removed without otherwise affecting the operation of the gun. The firing pin is an inertia type, and carrying the gun with the chamber loaded and the hammer fully down should be quite safe, but check to be sure that the firing pin retainer is tight (see the remarks on this in the section on the Colt 1911 pistol).

The P-35 Hi-Power is, of course, one of the very good ones.

Smith & Wesson Model 61 Pistol

When the GCA-68 banned the importation of small handguns, the people at Smith & Wesson hastened to put the final touches on their design for a new pocket pistol, the first of this type to be made by S&W since the demise of their .32 automatic in 1936. The new gun began as a .25 auto, but it was soon decided to make it in .22 Long Rifle chambering. When it emerged in 1970, it was designated the Model 61, and given the trade name of "Escort." For several reasons, the gun was not well-accepted, and it was withdrawn from production in 1973.

I think one of the main reasons for its failure was its external appearance. The basic design of this gun was borrowed from the Bayard Model 1908 pistol *(q.v.)*, and it may be that the early European recoil-spring-over-barrel arrangement was a bit too weird for the modern American shooter. Smith & Wesson made this same mistake once before when they used Belgian Charles Clement's design for their first automatic pistol in 1913. In the case of the Model 61, there were other negative points. In an era of double-action trigger systems and external hammers, this gun had a single-action trigger, and the hammer was fully enclosed by the frame and slide. The upper rear curve of the grip frame was much too shallow, setting the gun too high in the hand, and causing pronounced muzzle whip and a tendency to shoot low when quick-firing from the hip. Early in the production in May of 1970, S&W added a magazine safety to prevent firing when the magazine is removed. This little abomination is a formed piece of flat steel riveted inside the right wall of the magazine well and is tempered to be its own spring. It doesn't break, it's just a nuisance that renders the gun useless in a survival situation if the magazine is lost.

I have heard of, but have not ac-

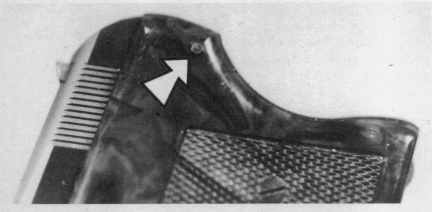

Arrow points to the hammer indicator, easily lost when the left grip is removed.

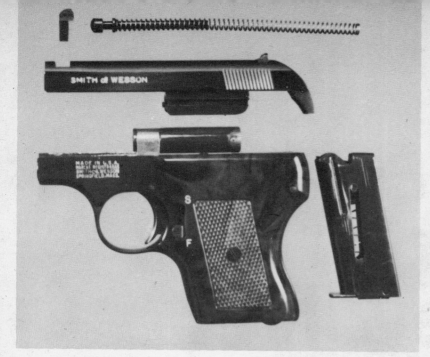

S&W Model 61 pistol, field-stripped. Note the small take-down block/front sight unit at upper left, a part that is easily lost.

tually examined, a case in which a prematurely detonated round forced the left sideplate, which is made of non-ferrous alloy, outward. If this did indeed happen, I think it should be viewed as a freak incident, as the gun is otherwise built with more than sufficient strength for years of normal use.

Aside from the replacement of an occasional firing pin broken by repeated dry-firing, the only repairs I've done with any regularity are the supply and installation of several parts that are easily lost when the shooter decides to dismantle the gun in the field. The takedown key is a block which locks into the recoil spring guide and also bears the front sight. The relatively small part can easily disappear in the tall grass. If the fingers slip during disassembly, the recoil spring guide can depart with considerable speed, powered by its long spring.

In the upper rear area of the left grip panel is a small button which is forced outward by the hammer when it is cocked. This indicator does not show whether the chamber is loaded, but it does tell, by sight or touch, that the hammer is back. The indicator button is retained only by the grip panel, and when the left grip is removed, the

button and its spring are easily lost. All parts are, of course, readily obtainable from S&W.

The Model 61 was beautifully made to Smith & Wesson's usual high standards and was reliable and accurate. It is now of more interest to collectors than shooters.

Removing the left grip exposes the safety lever and disconnector. Three screws retain the large sideplate which gives access to the internal mechanism.

The magazine safety (arrow), is a formed flat spring riveted inside the right wall of the magazine well.

Smith & Wesson Model 1878 Revolver

Made from 1878 to 1892, this .32 centerfire revolver was the first Smith & Wesson to have a rebounding hammer. It is a single-action gun with no trigger guard, the trigger being housed in a projection from the underside of the frame. This type is often called a "spur trigger" or "sheath trigger." The hammer rebound is accomplished in an unusual manner. The mainspring is a twin-hook stirrup type, and its mating stirrup-lever on the hammer is designed so that when the stirrup-bar is fully into the hooks, the hammer rests slightly back from the firing position. To travel all the way down to firing position, the stirrup-bar must climb partway out of the hooks, and after firing, the tension of the heavy mainspring causes it to drop back into them, raising the hammer to engage the safety step. It's an ingenious design, but it does put a strain on both the spring hooks and the stirrup-lever, and breakage is not unusual at this point.

In addition to the mainspring, flat springs are used at three other points in the design. The cylinder hand is powered by a narrow spring lying in a well in the front face of the hammer, and breakage is not usual except in careless disassembly. The cylinder stop spring has a loop at its forward end for passage of the bottom plate screw, and although it is not severly flexed in normal operation, it often cracks at the edge of the loop. The trigger spring is a flat V-type and does receive a good deal of compression. Breakage is frequent. All of these springs can be replaced with ones of doubled round wire, and this is fortunate, as parts are almost non-existent.

As in all top-break revolvers, the Model 1878 is subject to loosening of the barrel latch because of wear at the rear face of the latching lugs on the frame. This can be remedied by the method described in the section on the Smith & Wesson Model 1880 revolver—by drilling a small hole in the rear face of each lug, setting a hard steel pin in the holes and facing them off until the latch is snug.

The original grips of this gun are black molded hard rubber, and this material becomes brittle with age. No modern replacements are available, so if the grips are broken, new ones must be made. The original grips are fitted very tightly to the frame, and if removal is absolutely necessary, this should be done with extreme care. More of these are broken in removal

The top right arrow points to the engagement of the mainspring and hammer stirrup. Next is the cylinder hand spring in the front face of the hammer. Lower right arrow points toward the V-type trigger spring, and the lower arrow at the left indicates the location of the flat cylinder stop spring.

than in actual use of the gun.

Although this model is perfectly safe to shoot with modern .32 Smith & Wesson cartridges, the increasing number of S&W collectors makes it more valuable as a collector piece than as a practical revolver. Still, I know of several that are functioning as shooters.

Smith & Wesson Model 1880 Top-Break Revolver

At one point in American firearms history, nearly every arms maker in the nation was producing a top-break style revolver. As might be expected, Smith & Wesson made them best. Their .32 and .38 double-action top-break was introduced in 1880, and when production of the .38 ceased in 1911, around a half-million had been made. The .32 version lasted a bit longer, until 1919, and the total number was slightly lower, around 300 thousand. In comparsion to other revolvers of the same period and type, the Smith & Wessons were markedly superior in both materials and workmanship.

One ailment of these revolvers is shared with all other top-break guns: With age and long usage, the T-shaped barrel latch tends to loosen. The latch itself is not at fault. The actual cause is wear on the rear faces of the twin frame posts on which it locks. There are several ways to remedy this, but the best is to drill a $\frac{1}{16}$-inch hole about $\frac{5}{32}$-inch deep in each post, midway on the rear face, drive in tightly-fitted steel pins and file them off until the latch is tightened. When driving in the pins, be sure to firmly support the frame posts, to keep them from bending or breaking off. For another way of tightening the latch, see the pages covering the Iver-Johnson top-break revolver.

In the Model 1880 there are several trouble spots, most of which show up only after long, hard use. An exception to this, and the one thing which might be called a chronic ailment, is the cylinder stop. It is tempered to serve as its own spring, and at one point on its long shank it is very thin. Breakage at this point is frequent and presents a problem. Original parts are practically non-existent, no one has reproduced it commercially, and making a replacement to the original pattern is a tedious job, even for a good gunsmith. I have made this part from shaped, flat spring stock, substituting a hollow arc for the solid portion of the original. It doesn't look right, but it works and will last longer.

The trigger guard is spring-tempered and has a retaining lip at front and rear which holds it in the frame by its own tension. One leaf of the V-type trigger spring bears on the trigger guard. If the guard spring tension has weakened, pulling the trigger can cause the rear lip of the guard to jump out of the frame. The trigger guard can be re-shaped and retempered, but this is a job for the gunsmith.

The arrows point to the location of four blade-type springs that are susceptible to breakage or weakening. They power the trigger, cylinder hand, hammer and sear.

The hammer was originally surface-hardened, and the sear was made with only normal heat treatment, so the sear is more likely to wear and fail to hold the hammer back for single-action firing. A worn sear beak can be built up with steel weld, recut to shape, and rehardened by any good gunsmith. Welding is not always necessary. If the wear is not too great, a simple recutting to restore the sharp edge of the sear beak will do it.

The trigger, sear, and cylinder hand springs are known to break with some frequency, the hammer spring less often. All four of these are blade-type, and some are flexed rather severely. The sear and trigger springs can be replaced with doubled round wire, but this method is not adaptable to the hammer and cylinder hand springs. The hammer spring, however, can be replaced by an altered replacement mainspring for the S&W Military & Police revolver, and these are available everywhere and still made by the factory.

The grips, if they are factory-original, will likely be either black hard rubber or genuine mother-of-pearl. They are relatively fragile, in either case, but the pearl grips are especially prone to breakage. Even a slight over-tightening of the grip screw can crack them, and I have known them to break from recoil when the gun was fired. Excellent replacements are made by Scott, Sile, and others, and these are much more durable than the originals.

If you own an original Model 1880 in excellent, like-new condition, it would be best if you didn't shoot it at all. A serious Smith & Wesson collector will often pay enough for it to cover the cost of something more modern.

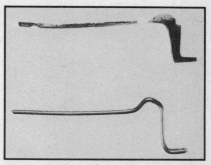

Original parts are almost nonexistent; however, replacement parts can be made. A broken original cylinder stop (top) is compared to a replacement fabricated from flat spring stock.

Wear on the barrel latch area of the frame is common to all top-break guns. It can be tightened by the installation of steel pins which serve to replace the worn rear surface (arrow) of the frame lugs.

The S&W Model 1880's sear beak (arrow) is subject to wear or chipping and can cause a malfunction. The beak itself can be built up with weld, cut to shape and rehardened by a competent gunsmith.

Smith & Wesson Model 19 Revolver

Essentially, the Model 19 is simply a .38 Masterpiece with an ejector-rod shroud and the extra heat treatment to handle .357 Magnum pressures. Being on the medium "K" frame, its 35-ounce weight and adjustable sights have made it very much in demand by police officers, security agents and shooters in general. During our military endeavors in southeast Asia, it saw much unofficial use by the men in the field, who found that oriental body armor which stopped the .45 auto was no proof against the .357 Magnum round.

The Model 19 began production in January of 1956, and serial numbering started with K260000. (We'll take a brief time-out here, while you check to see whether your gun is one of the earliest numbers.) This gun is another of those that make a poor subject for troubleshooting, as hardly anything ever goes wrong with it. As always, though, there are one or two points to watch out for if only in the area of good preventive maintenance.

On the Model 19, as on all Smith & Wesson revolvers of recent manufacture, the ejector rod has a left-hand thread for attachment. In other words, to unscrew it, you turn it to the right, or clockwise (as viewed from the front of the gun). Since the S&W cylinder rotates in the same direction, any slight friction on the rod tends to tighten it—a good design feature. Even so, the rod may occasionally loosen, either from heavy-load vibration or insufficient torque during reassembly. When this occurs, the rod can edge forward, and even a small distance is enough to bring its hollow tip onto the forward locking bolt to such an extent that the cylinder latch will no longer release.

This is easily correctable, of course, by simply tightening the rod. It could be embarrassing, though, if it occurs when you are trying to reload during a serious social encounter. So, it's a good idea to check the rod for tightness occasionally. If, while holding the cylinder, the rod can be turned easily by the fingers, it's loose. To tighten it, remove the crane and cylinder from the gun by backing out the forward sideplate screw and separate the crane and cylinder. With a piece of thick leather or two blocks of soft wood to protect the rod from marring, grip it lightly in a vise. Insert two or three empty cartridge cases in the chambers to prevent strain on the ejector arms and spline, and turn the

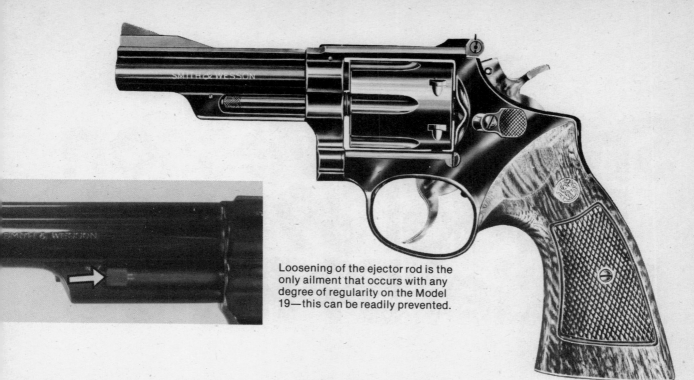

Loosening of the ejector rod is the only ailment that occurs with any degree of regularity on the Model 19—this can be readily prevented.

cylinder to the left, with hand pressure only, to tighten the rod. Be careful not to overdo it—just get it snug.

The Model 19 has no other quirks that can cause trouble. Like most Smith & Wessons, it seems to go on working forever. The only actual repair I have ever done on this gun was in a case where someone had pried off the sideplate, warping it to the extent that it was binding the internal parts when it was put back and the screws tightened. The proper method of removal is to take out the sideplate screws, then tap the grip frame with a wooden, leather, or plastic mallet until the plate loosens and drops off. Before this, of course, you have had the good sense to remove the crane, cylinder, and grips.

Smith & Wesson sideplates are so carefully fitted that it is unwise to remove them unless absolutely necessary, and routine cleaning does not require it. One final note regarding "fine tuning" of the Model 19 to lighten the double-action trigger pull: Some gunsmiths, who should know better, put a slight "kink" in the hammer spring to achieve lighter tension. This has the desired effect, but it makes the flat mainspring prone to breakage and produces a change in direction of force on the hammer stirrup, resulting in a "loading" of the spring near the double-action let-off point. To properly lighten the pull, you remove a very small amount from the tip of the hammer spring strain screw, remove a coil or two from the rebound slide spring and put a mirror polish on all of the bearing surfaces in the system. Actually, it's a job best left to a competent gunsmith. If you make the mainspring tension too light, you'll get occasional misfires, and in an emergency situation, this could be very hazardous to your health.

Jan Stevenson, whose opinions I greatly respect, has said that the Model 19, "Comes closer than any other to being the all-around, all-purpose handgun." If we're talking about revolvers only, I agree with him.

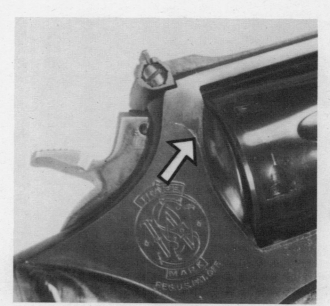

The arrow points to a slight burr where the sideplate meets the frame—evidence that someone pried the plate up during previous disassembly rather than tapping it free.

Smith & Wesson Model 39 and Model 59 Pistols

Until August of 1954, the shooter who wanted a pistol in 9mm Luger chambering with a double-action trigger system had no choice—it was the Walther P-38 or nothing. At this point, along came Smith & Wesson with an excellent alternative. It was smaller, much lighter, and had all of the capabilities of the P-38, plus a horizontally adjustable rear sight and much better balance. It was designated the Model 39, and a few pistols were also made without the double-action system—10 of them to be exact. This experimental version was called the Model 44, and you are not likely to see one. During the regular production run, a small number were turned out with steel frames rather than the usual alloy. These are rare, and, when found, are expensive. Nearly 20 years after the debut of the Model 39, the Smith & Wesson designers put the icing on the cake, in a manner of speaking, by bringing out the Model 59. From the frame up, it was a Model 39—in fact, the slide assemblies will interchange. At the bottom, though, was a redesigned grip frame, including a stagger-type, 15-round magazine. I was fortunate to be the writer of the first actual field-test of this gun. I liked it then, and today, several

thousand rounds later, I still do. The straight-backed grip frame of the Model 59 feels better in my hand than the arched back of the Model 39, but this is strictly a *personal* preference. Since the internal mechanisms are virtually identical, most of the comments that follow will apply to both guns.

The manual safety is a variation of the Walther system, rolling shoulders of solid steel upward to shield the firing pin head from the hammer face, while immobilizing the firing pin. As in the Walther, the last fraction of the safety-lever arc activates a sear-trip, dropping the hammer. I have never understood the purpose or value of the hammer-drop feature, and since it can be cancelled by the removal of a single part, I have often made this change on my own gun and for numerous others who asked for it. The sear release lever can be put back, if it's ever wanted.

Another part that is often removed, even more frequently than the one mentioned above, is the ejector depressor plunger, and its spring. Taking out this little assembly, located under the rear sight, cancels the magazine safety and allows the gun to be fired with the magazine removed. In a survival situation with a lost maga-

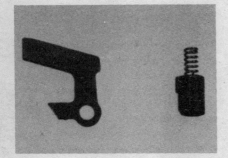

Two parts which many shooters remove from the Model 39 and Model 59 pistols. The automatic hammer drop (left), and the magazine safety plunger and spring (right).

136

Smith & Wesson Model 59 pistol.

Smith & Wesson
Model 39 pistol

zine, this could be an important consideration. Again, the part and spring can be saved, and later put back, if desired.

Breaking a long-held tradition, several police forces adopted the Model 39 as their standard side arm, and one of these was the Illinois State Police. It was soon found that a freak occurrence in re-holstering the gun could cause partial disassembly. The slide stop shaft protruded rather prominently from the right side of the frame to make disassembly easier. If the slide happened to be forced back a certain distance as the gun was holstered, and the inside of the holster pressed against the slide stop shaft, it could be pushed over enough to disengage the slide stop from the frame. An unlikely sequence, but it did happen at least once, and Smith & Wesson quickly reduced the length of the slide stop shaft. Previous to this, another change had been made in the basic design. The extractor was originally tempered to be its own heavy blade spring, and this was soon replaced by a conventional pivoting extractor with a separate coil spring. Less likely to break, and less expensive to make, the new extractor is a good change.

Some of the early pistols had a fairly steep feed ramp and had some difficulty with several of the new high-performance 9mm loads having soft or hollow-point bullets. Ironically, some of the most frequent jams occurred with an excellent but very stubby round made by—Smith & Wesson! Again, the factory was quick to alter the feed ramp from that point in the production.

The Model 39 and Model 59 pistols have no chronic trouble spots, and in the event of something routine, such as a broken firing pin, parts are readily available.

Photo on the right shows a Model 39 with the older, longer slide latch (arrow). To the left is a photo of a Model 59 with the newer, shorter slide latch now common to both models. The slide latch is the key to takedown and on the older models the protruding latch has, on occasion, been inadvertently pushed out as the gun was holstered. What you can end up with is a partially field-stripped Model 39 or 59— not much fun in a fire fight.

Smith & Wesson .35 Automatic

When the grand old firm of Smith & Wesson decided to enter the field of pocket automatics, they made two serious errors. First, they used a basic design that was originated by Charles P. Clement of Belgium —a design that worked quite well in smaller calibers, but was not suited to larger rounds. Secondly, they chambered the pistol for a weird new cartridge called the .35 Smith & Wesson Automatic—a lead bullet having a jacketed nose. The ".35" designation was for advertising purposes only, to set it apart from the well-known .32 auto round. Actual bullet diameter was .312 to .318, while the standard .32 auto measured .303 to .312. It is possible to shoot .32 auto rounds in the .35 Smith & Wesson pistol, but the cases will bulge alarmingly. The original .35 rounds are now in the realm of the cartridge collector and are too valuable to shoot.

The S&W .35 automatic pistol was made from 1913 to 1921, the last pistol leaving the factory in January of that year with a total of 8,350 having been produced. Three factors hastened the demise of this design. The modified Clement design looked very European, and conservative American gun buyers disliked its strange appearance. Its price was somewhat higher than its contemporary competitors, and many stores failed to stock the odd cartridge.

To compensate for the use of a small, light breech block in conjunction with a medium-powered cartridge, S&W used a very strong recoil spring. So strong, in fact, that anyone with less strength than King Kong will find it impossible to retract the breech block for loading the first round. To circumvent this, they designed a latch on the breech block which, when pushed through from left to right, disengaged the little "slide" from the recoil spring. It worked perfectly, but to anyone unfamiliar with the pistol, it was tricky.

Two manual safety catches were provided: a tiny serrated "wheel," located inconveniently in the left upper curve of the backstrap; and a grip-type catch (a small one-finger pedal), located just below the trigger guard on the right side of the frontstrap. The grip safety was subject to catching on pocket edges and if bent or broken off would make firing impossible. I have seen several of these guns in which this little abomination had been entirely removed, much to the chagrin of today's collectors.

After the grip screw is removed, grip panels slide downward off the frame. Grips are often damaged by amateur attempts to pry them outward from the side.

Smith & Wesson .35 automatic. A total of 8,350 of these were made.

The .32 Smith & Wesson automatic. Exactly 957 of these were produced—a real collector's find.

There are only two flat springs in the design. The sear is powered by a rather heavy blade-type, barely flexed in normal operation and not prone to breakage. The trigger guard, the key to the takedown, is also tempered to be its own locking spring and is heavy enough that it is not subject to breakage in normal use.

The pistol is marvelously complicated, having 62 separate parts, some of them tiny and delicate. Only the legendary quality of Smith & Wesson materials and workmanship saved it from being a mechanical disaster. The grip panels are one area in which amateur removal frequently causes damage. After taking out the single retaining screw at the lower edge, some have attempted to pry the grips off to the side, with disastrous results. The fine walnut grips are riveted to a flat steel

A field-stripped .32 S&W. The design was somewhat simplified, but not enough.

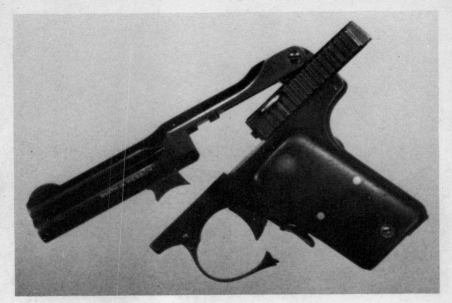

The .35 S&W, partially field-stripped. Removal of the hinge screw allows the barrel and spring housing to be taken off, and the breech block can then be lifted off the frame.

Arrow indicates the second-finger, pedal-type grip safety. It was not one of Smith & Wesson's better ideas.

plate, its front and rear edges fitting tightly under ledges on the grip frame. For removal, the grip panels must be slid downward. No replacements are available, and this also applies to other parts.

In 1924, Smith & Wesson redesigned the pistol and kept only the general design and the disengagement latch on the breech block. This was really unnecessary, as the new gun had a full-weight moving slide. The odd cartridge was abandoned, the new chambering being for the popular .32 automatic round. The little wheel safety was omitted, but the pedal-type grip safety was retained. Gone were the multiple curves and grooves of the exterior, replaced by neat flat planes. It was a very nice pistol but still complicated and expensive to manufacture. The Colt Automatic of that time sold for $20.50, while the Smith & Wesson was priced at $33.50, a princely sum in those days. It was discontinued in 1927 and last sold around 1936. Exactly 957 of these were made, and locating one can bring a manic gleam to the eyes of any collector of Smith & Wesson guns or automatic pistols.

Hi-Standard Model 101 Duramatic

Designed to be the "economy" model of the High Standard line of .22 automatics, the Duramatic has several interesting features, one of which is the absence of a grip frame. The one-piece grip is made of heavy plastic, attached to the main frame by a single large bolt. This system not only saves production costs, but also affects the weight distribution, giving a slight muzzle-heaviness that many shooters like.

The pistol's only serious chronic ailment is breakage of the striker sleeve screw. The striker sleeve, which is also the base for the striker and recoil springs, is mounted on the frame with a single small countersunk screw. The sleeve is not shelved or otherwise supported against the pressure on its forward end, and all of the strain of spring compression bears on that single screw. When the screw breaks, it is difficult to repair, as you have a steel screw broken off in an alloy frame.

Aside from pressure breakage, the screw can also be fractured by improper disassembly. About a ¼-inch into the frame, there is a cross-pin which contacts a groove in the screw to prevent its loosen-ing. If the screw is removed without first taking out this pin, the screw will break at the groove, below the frame surface, and this will be even more difficult to repair.

A broken striker sleeve screw can be replaced with a new original type from High Standard, as all replacement parts are available directly from the company. When I do this repair, though, I take steps to strengthen the system. First, the cross-pin is removed. Then, a sharp-pointed tool and a

Arrow points to the frame hole where a cross-pin locks the striker sleeve screw. Forceps hold a replacement screw showing the lock pin groove on its side.

small hammer are used to back out the broken end of the screw from the frame. Next, the frame is drilled and retapped for a screw of slightly larger diameter, with its head reduced to fit the countersink in the sleeve. To give extra support, a 3/16-inch steel pin is set into the frame, just to the rear of the screw, with its top protruding to enter a hole in the underside of the striker sleeve. This gives a two-point support, and none of the pistols I've altered this way have had any more trouble.

In normal operation, there is no other quirk in the Model 101 that causes trouble, but there is one thing that should be mentioned, and this applies to almost any gun, not just this one: Some shooters have the bad habit of pulling hard on the trigger while the safety is in the "safe" position. In the Dura-matic, as in several other pistols, the safety blocks the sear, and the trigger and trigger bar are of very light, slim construction. With extreme pressure on the trigger, it is possible to break either the trigger or the rear tip of the trigger bar. This, of course, can easily be avoided.

The Model 101 Duramatic was also made for Sears as the J. C. Higgins Model 80.

Hi-Standard Sentinel Revolver

The High Standard Company has long been known for a line of excellent and moderately-priced .22 automatic pistols. In 1955, they offered a .22 revolver called the Sentinel. Its swing-out cylinder and nine-shot capacity quickly made it a favorite with campers, trappers and casual plinkers. Other good points in the design were a rebounding hammer with safety-block and a very comfortable grip. The gun was also made for Sears under the J.C. Higgins name.

The arrow to the left points to the cylinder stop spring, shown with the hollow crane pivot over its end. The arrow to the right points to the narrow frame bridge behind the trigger where breakage occurs on early guns. The one shown is the later, stronger version.

During the past 22 years of its production, High Standard has modified and improved the design. One of the main changes was a new grip frame. On the earliest models, the grip frame had a very narrow section just to the rear of the trigger on each side, and it was prone to breakage at that point. The present frames are thicker in that area, and I've seen no breakage in these. There have also been changes in the trigger spring and cylinder hand spring, and both are definite improvements.

The only real trouble spot in the Sentinel involves the part called the "link pivot pin"—actually, the crane pivot and the cylinder stop spring. The spring extends forward into the hollow pivot, and to the rear, surrounds the tail of the cylinder stop. The proper tension of this spring is critical to the functioning of the cylinder stop. As long as everything is in original condition, the system works perfectly. If the spring is weakened from long use or, more likely, deformed by amateur disassembly, it can cause jamming of the cylinder stop and trigger. Similar trouble can occur if dirt or a burr on the crane should prevent full forward travel of the pivot, causing a decided increase in the ten-

sion of the cylinder stop spring.

Any of the conditions mentioned above can be easily corrected, of course. In most cases, simply installing a new, factory original spring will put it back in good shooting order. When the new spring is installed, care should be taken to see that the end which enters the frame goes into the tail of the cylinder stop, or the new spring will be deformed. Also, during reassembly, be sure that the cylinder hand spring on the right side of the grip frame does not slip out of its recess in the cylinder hand, or it may be deformed by the edge of the main frame.

Replacement parts are no problem, as they are still available from High Standard. In the case of the early revolvers which may have a broken grip frame at the narrow point, you can purchase the few parts that will convert it to the stronger current type. I have had some success at rejoining broken old-style grip frames, but welding aluminum alloy is extremely tricky. If your Sentinel is a later one, you won't have to worry about this.

When reassembling, be sure the cylinder hand spring (arrow) is hooked into its step on the right side of the hand.

Hi-Standard Model HD Pistol

The Hi-Standard Model HDM pistol shown (above) is the postwar commercial version with the 6¾-inch barrel.

The Model HD and the wartime-introduced HDM (which differs mainly in the addition of a manual safety) are around in great numbers, even though they were made for a relatively short time—from 1941 to 1951. With their good grip angle, good balance, heavy barrel and outside hammer, they have always been popular as an intermediate target pistol. During WW II, the Model HD was slightly re-designed for military practice use, and this gun became the HDM.

Aside from its good handling qualities, the Model HD also has a reputation for reliability, a thing of some importance when considering the inherent feeding problems of the .22 Long Rifle cartridge. Like most of the early High Standard pistols, the HD has twin tempered spring "fingers" at the top of its magazine which lightly grip the cartridge as it is picked up and moved by the slide, releasing it only after its nose is well-aligned with the chamber. It may be that this system is one reason for the lack of feed and ejection problems.

The main source of difficulty with the Model HD involves the

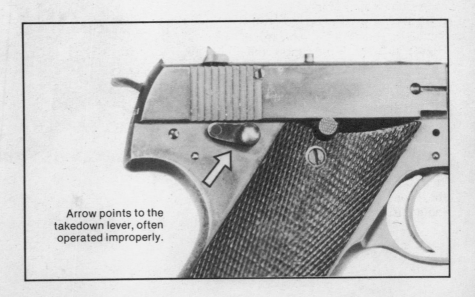

Arrow points to the takedown lever, often operated improperly.

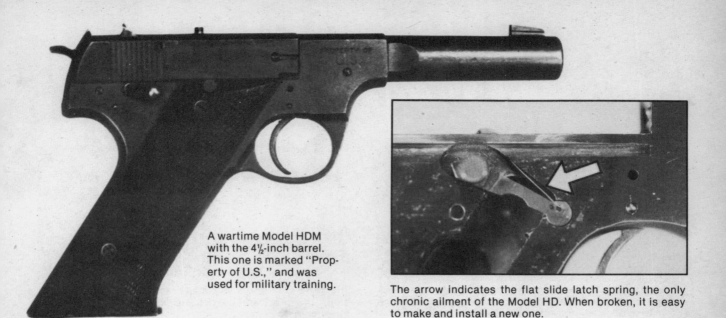

A wartime Model HDM with the 4½-inch barrel. This one is marked "Property of U.S.," and was used for military training.

The arrow indicates the flat slide latch spring, the only chronic ailment of the Model HD. When broken, it is easy to make and install a new one.

takedown system, both from breakage and operational error. Inside the top of the frame there is a small pivoting block with a projection at top left that forms the base for the recoil spring, while the entire block serves as a backstop for the slide. Factory lists call this part the "slide stop." It is connected to a lever on the right rear of the grip frame, and after the recoil spring is compressed and locked by a button on top of the slide, the takedown lever is pushed downward to tip over the "slide stop," allowing the slide to be removed to the rear of the frame.

Quite often, someone who is unfamiliar with the gun will turn the takedown lever without first locking the spring, an action that is difficult but not impossible. As a result, the entire system can be jammed and the recoil spring and other parts deformed. When this happens, it will usually be necessary to consult a gunsmith. If the takedown lever shaft is twisted or broken, repair will not be easy, and parts are available only occasionally from used-parts dealers.

The "slide stop" block is also known to crack during normal operation, especially if the recoil spring has weakened after long use and high velocity cartridges are used. The break will usually occur either on a level with the top of the frame or at the lower edge in the pivot loops. When I repair this, I always use a slightly heavier piece of steel and a torsion-type spring, doing away with the coil spring and plunger that originally kept the block in position. Where the plunger contacts the front face of the block there is a recess for the plunger head, making a weak point at a location where strength is needed. Any competent gunsmith can make a replacement "slide stop" that will last a lot longer.

There are a few blade-type springs in the design, and the one that seems to break most frequently is the one that powers the slide latch, located inside the top of the right grip panel. This is a simple, straight flat spring and is not difficult to make or replace. The slide latch, which holds the slide open when the last shot is fired, is held in place by the grip panel, so when the grip is off, be careful this part isn't lost.

The trigger bar/disconnector, which lies behind a removable plate on the left side of the gun, is

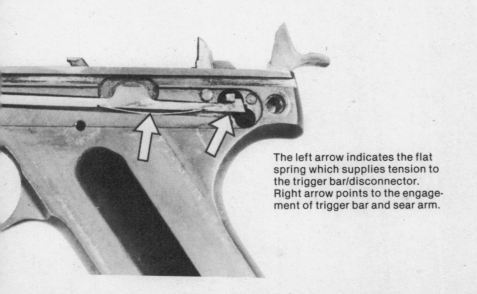

The left arrow indicates the flat spring which supplies tension to the trigger bar/disconnector. Right arrow points to the engagement of trigger bar and sear arm.

Arrow indicates the "slide stop," the pivoting steel block which is both slide retainer and recoil spring base. The one shown is an original—they often break.

The arrow points to a handmade replacement for the "slide stop," this one made heavier and with a different spring arrangement for better strength.

also powered by a flat spring, but this one is barely flexed in normal operation and rarely breaks. Here, again, the spring is a simple piece of tempered flat stock with a slight curve and easy to reproduce. The trigger bar itself has an L-shaped hook at the rear which engages a left lateral projection on the sear. Both the trigger bar and the sear arm have been known to break, and in this case, repair could get a little expensive unless used parts can be found.

On the wartime and postwar HDM, which has a manual safety lever, the lever is retained by a stepped screw which is set tightly into the frame, its larger portion forming the pivot for the lever. When wear occurs beneath the flange of the screw head or in the corresponding well in the safety lever, this part can loosen, and tightening of the screw will not help. To snug it up, a very small amount of steel must be turned from the lower face of the screw, next to the rebated and threaded portion.

Menta Pistol

The trigger bar spring (arrow) is the only flat spring found in the Menta—breakage is rare. Note the open left side of the frame where the grip is without central support along its entire length. Because of this the grip is susceptible to breaking.

There are four almost identical pistols in this group, each bearing a different name. You may have seen a gun much like the one shown, but marked "Beholla," "Stenda," or "Leonhardt." The Beholla came first, its name derived from a combination of Becker & Hollander, the firm that designed and produced it around 1908. The gun was later made under license by the other three firms.

The basic design of this pistol is excellent from the standpoint of a single-action, striker-fired handgun. One wonders why it wasn't more successful. It's just a little smaller than most of its 7.65mm contemporaries, and the grip angle is good. In the Menta version, one chronic ailment of striker-type pistols is made less likely: The striker point is of much larger diameter, reducing the crystallization factor. I have never seen one of these with a broken firing pin point. The sear system is well-designed, giving a very smooth trigger pull. The takedown system is extremely simple, and the external surfaces of the pistol are flat and uncluttered in keeping with its intended use as a pocket gun. The extractor is large, strong, and well-shaped. Finally, there is only one flat spring in the design, supplying tension to the trigger bar/disconnector. This spring is not subjected to extreme flexing and rarely breaks.

There are very few points for criticism. The grips are old-style hard rubber and are secured by a single screw at their rear center edge. The left grip is centrally unsupported for its entire length and is susceptible to breakage. Another point that could be mentioned is the trigger bar which has enough side play to allow it to slip out of engagement with the sear lever if the trigger is pulled while the magazine is removed. This quirk is not present in all of these pistols, and when it occurs, it is easily correctable. The safety catch is a little unhandy to operate. Located just to the rear of the left grip top, it swings back and upward to firing position, a less than convenient motion. The safety does, however, act directly on the sear.

In the event that a part may be broken or missing, it will usually have to be made because the only thing that has been commercially reproduced is the magazine. There is a slight possibility that the used-parts dealers may occasionally have certain parts.

Whether your pistol is marked Menta, Stenda, Leonhardt, or Beholla, you have a well-designed and dependable pocket automatic, handicapped only by its lack of an external hammer and double-action trigger system.

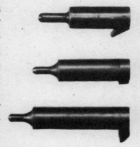

When compared to others, the Menta's firing pin (top) is a sturdy one. The firing tip is heavy and seldom, if ever, breaks.

Tokarev Model T-33 Pistol

Around 1925, when Fedor V. Tokarev designed the first Russian military automatic pistol, he borrowed freely from existing designs. When the gun was produced in 1930, it had the general shape of the Browning Model 1903 pistol and the locking system of the U.S. Model 1911. Major Tokarev's own contribution, however, was very important—a unique "package" firing system, an easily removable sub-frame containing the hammer, sear, disconnector, ejector, and the necessary springs. This system was soon thereafter used by Charles Gabriel Petter in the French Model 1935A pistol.

At the time the Tokarev origi-nated, Russia did not have extensive machining capabilities, so the pistol was designed for ease of manufacturing. It has no complicated mechanisms and is very strong and trouble-free. The trigger, disconnector, and sear are powered by flat springs, but these are not flexed greatly in normal use, and seldom break.

In fact, the only things that break with any degree of regularity are the grips. These are retained on the frame by pivoting plates of flat steel, and they are centrally unsupported. They are also made of a resin-based plastic which is extremely brittle, and replacements are almost impossible to find.

Pulling the disassembly latch by its rear tab can break the grip if your tool slips. Use a brass or aluminum tool—an old key works well—and push it from the front.

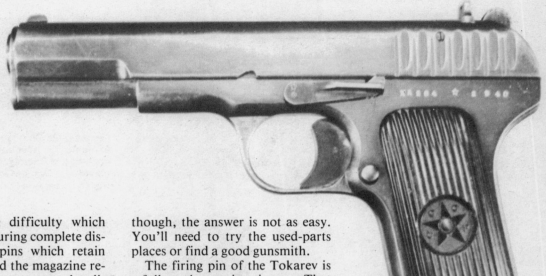

There is one difficulty which shows up only during complete disassembly. The pins which retain the firing pin and the magazine release button have tempered split ends with flanges that fit into recesses and hold the pins in place. If you try to drive out these pins in the usual way, the tempered ends will usually break. The right tool, which is easy to make, must be of the same diameter as the pins and have a V-shaped tip to compress the flanges out of their recesses. If this advice comes too late, and breakage has already occurred, an ordinary fitted pin can be used to retain the firing pin. If the magazine release button is broken,

though, the answer is not as easy. You'll need to try the used-parts places or find a good gunsmith.

The firing pin of the Tokarev is a full-reach, non-inertia type. That is, when the hammer is completely down, the point of the firing pin will protrude from the breech face. If a round is in the chamber, the point will be resting against its primer, a dangerous situation, especially if the gun is dropped. The hammer does have a safety step, and there is a tab on the disconnector which locks the slide when the hammer is in that position. Even so, a sharp blow on the hammer or the muzzle can override this system. I know of one instance

of this happening. There is, however, a simple way to make this system less hazardous. Just remove around $\frac{1}{16}$- to $\frac{3}{32}$-inch from the point of the firing pin and re-round it to shape. This will effec-

Arrows point to the tempered split-end pins that retain the firing pin (top) and magazine release (bottom). To drift them out, a special tool is required.

Arrow points to the pivoting lockplate that retains the left grip. The grips are of rather fragile plastic and lack central support—they are subject to breakage.

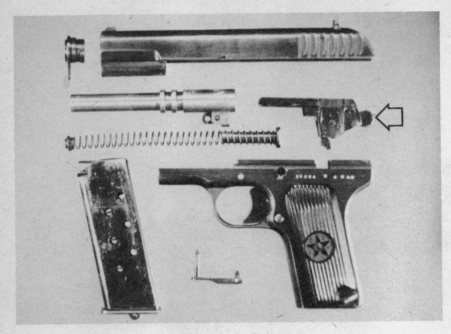

(Left) When field-stripped, the simplicity of the Tokarev can be seen. The sub-frame (arrow) contains the complete firing system.

(Below) This Chinese Communist Type 51 pistol is, mechanically, an exact copy of the Tokarev. Many Soviet influenced or dominated countries have their own version of the "Tokarev."

tively convert it to an inertia-type. Occasionally, with some hard-primer European cartridges, it may also be necessary to install a slightly heavier hammer spring.

Speaking of cartridges, the original 7.62mm Tokarev pistol round is practically identical to the 7.63mm Mauser (.30 Mauser) cartridge, which, unfortunately, was recently discontinued by U.S. manufacturers. The Mauser round works perfectly in most Tokarev pistols, but it's now very difficult to find, and the foreign surplus stuff is also disappearing. If you want to shoot a Tokarev extensively, you'll have to locate those fired cases in the tall grass and become a handloader. If you do handload, however, Hardin Specialty Distributors (P.O. Box 338, Radcliff, KY 40160) has recently introduced brass for this cartridge that's reformed from .223 cases. Price is around $4.20 per 50 at this writing.

The Radom P-35 VIS pistol can be found in various forms as dictated by its period of manufacture. This "Radom" is an early Nazi Occupation type.

Radom Pistol

The names to remember are Wilniewczyc and Skrzypinski. In 1935, the government of Poland selected their design to be the new side arm of the Polish Military Forces. Production of the pistol was assigned to Fabryka Broni, the Government Small Arms Factory at Radom. Although the pistol was officially named the "VIS Model 35," it soon came to be known by the name of the arsenal that produced it. While purist collectors may insist on calling it the "VIS," I always refer to it in print as the Radom. This may be technically wrong, but at least I have the satisfaction of knowing that almost everyone else will instantly recognize which pistol I'm talking about. The Radom was made from 1936 to 1939 by the Polish government, and from 1939 to 1945 production was continued under the Nazi Occupation. From the earliest government production to the very last Occupation guns, there was a marked deterioration in quality with many shortcuts in mechanical detail toward the end.

The designers borrowed heavily from two Browning designs, the U.S. Model 1911 and the Browning HP. The Radom has an external resemblance to the 1911, and the firing mechanism is very simi-

lar, but the barrel locking system is like the Hi-Power. There are also two points that are quite original—one good, one not so good. On the left rear of the slide is a lever, which, when rotated downward, pulls the firing pin inside its tunnel in the slide and in the last fraction of its arc drops the hammer. This is an ingenious way to lower the hammer with one hand after loading the chamber. It works perfectly and is quite safe to use, but only if the parts involved are original to the pistol. If someone has replaced the firing pin with one of different dimensions watch out. I have seen stories claiming that some Nazi ordnance people intentionally installed longer firing pins in Radom pistols with the idea that a soldier surrendering his pistol could trip the hammer drop and shoot his captor without touching the trigger. As in most of these stories, I think someone's imagination was working overtime.

Some writers have referred to the hammer drop lever as a safety. Once and for all, let's get it straight. The Radom has only one safety—the grip safety at the rear of the frame. The lever on the side of the frame which occupies the same space as the safety on the Model 1911 is not a safety at all,

Somewhat of a rarity, this Radom P-35 VIS is the original Polish version and, when compared to the others, is decidedly the best one a collector or shooter can find. Fit, finish and attention to detail are excellent. This version of the "Radom" is a little harder to come by as fewer were made and existing specimens are more in the collector's realm.

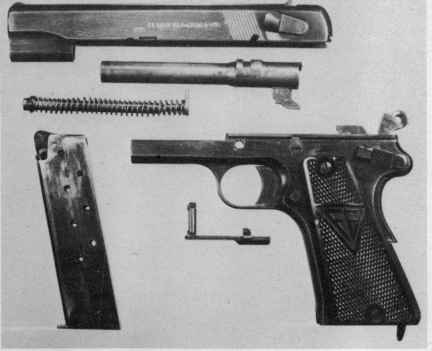

A Radom pistol, field-stripped. Note the captive recoil spring.

it's a dismounting lever. Its purpose is to hold the slide in position for easy removal of the slide stop during the takedown procedure. On very late wartime pistols, the dismounting lever was omitted, making takedown interesting for those of us with fewer than three hands.

The other original point in the design, the one that is not as desirable, is the recoil spring assembly. It is, in fact, the only weak point in the gun. The assembly features a captive spring—a good point. It accomplishes this, however, by having a smaller diameter rod pinned to the main spring guide which is hollowed to receive the smaller rod. The smaller rod, at the rear of the assembly, ends in a flat plate which bears on the underlug of the barrel, and also supplies tension, via an internal spring, to the slide stop. A long slot is cut into the smaller rod to allow it movement on its retaining pin, and the amount of steel left above and below the slot is rather small. This makes a fragile part, and one that is subjected to somewhat rigorous action during the recoil cycle. These break with some regularity, and while most parts for the Radom are usually available, this particular one is in short supply. When I replace these, I change the original design by using a solid rod, cutting a slight recess for staked retention, and doing away with the cross-pin. After this change is made, the Radom will go on working forever, except for routine replacement of such things as a broken firing pin or a weak spring.

There are two flat springs in the design. The extractor is tempered to be its own spring, but, like the one in the Model 1911 and the early Browning HP, this is a heavy part, and breakage is rare. The other blade spring is a three-

This Radom P-35 VIS pistol is a very late Nazi Occupation type. The takedown latch has been entirely eliminated and the solid-steel cross-pins replaced with pins made of rolled sheet steel. Also note the different grips.

The recoil spring unit has a separate spring-powered end-piece (right arrow) which operates the slide latch. This end-piece is cross-pinned (left arrow) to the main guide. This particular arrangement is the only weak point in the entire design.

fingered combination, much like the one in the Colt pistol, supplying tension to the sear, trigger/disconnector, and grip safety. Breakage is unusual, but there is often some weakening of the arm that powers the grip safety. In most cases, this can be corrected by reshaping, and this is a job for a gunsmith.

Original grips will be molded hard rubber, plastic or wood, depending on the age of the pistol. The grips are retained by two screws on each side, supported well by the frame, and are not usually susceptible to breakage. Commercial replacements are, however, available.

Once that little weak spot in the recoil spring unit is corrected, the Radom is one of the very good ones. For a military pistol, this gun is surprisingly accurate.

Thumb lever on the slide (upper arrow) retracts the firing pin and drops the hammer. The lever on the frame (lower arrow) is a slide latch used only during takedown. The grip safety is the only one provided in the Radom design.

Glisenti Pistol

This pistol had its beginning in a design by two Belgians named Haensler and Roch, who made a few experimental prototypes in Liege. On June 30, 1905, the design was patented in Italy by the Societa Siderurgica Glisenti, and the pistol was adopted by the Italian Army in 1906. These early guns were chambered for the 7.65mm Luger cartridge, and in 1910 the chambering was changed to 9mm Luger, but with a special Italian version of this round that had considerably lower pressure than other loadings. In the new chambering, the pistol was adopted for use by the Italian Army and Navy as the Pistola Automatica M. 1910. In 1911, the Metallurgica Bresciana Tempini, successor to the Glisenti firm, made a few slight changes in the design and marketed the altered pistol under the name "Brixia." In both forms, the pistol was made until around 1914.

The Glisenti is a handsome pistol, with flat, uncluttered planes on the sides and an appearance akin to the Luger. It sits well in the hand and has good pointing qualities, but the high placement of the bolt causes considerable muzzle whip in firing. The magazine is particularly outstanding, having open sides and serrated surfaces on the follower, allowing the follower to be easily drawn downward when loading. The fit and finish are very good, and the internal surfaces of the frame and sideplate are often pattern engine-turned. The manual safety is ingenious and positive, consisting of a device at the rear of the bolt that resembles a wing-nut. When rotated to the left, the safety turns a lug into a recess on the striker, locking it in cocked position. There is also a grip-type safety, located in the frontstrap of the grip frame, which blocks the trigger.

In examining this design, it would almost seem that the internal mechanism was worked out piecemeal. One can imagine a designer saying to his associate, "Oh, that doesn't work? Then we'll add a lever and spring *here* . . ." The Glisenti is full of blade-type springs and intricately shaped little parts. If I listed all the things that can go wrong, there'd be no space left for the photos in this section. I'll just try to point out the main deficiencies and say at the start that this pistol can be dangerous with full-power 9mm Luger cartridges.

The breech block, or bolt, is retained in the barrel extension by a

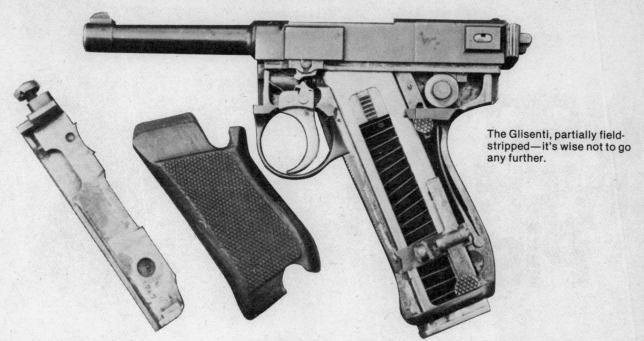

The Glisenti, partially field-stripped—it's wise not to go any further.

single cross-key of unheroic proportions. If it were not for the fact that this is a locked-breech pistol, breakage of the bolt retaining bar would likely have been a regular thing. If the cross-key should break, you'd have a close view of the rear end of the bolt—a very close view, just before it hits you in the eye! Fortunately, the heavy pivoting locking block requires the bolt to use up considerable energy in overcoming its spring-buffered engagement, so the retaining bar rarely breaks. Beware, however, of the Glisenti with a very weak locking block spring, or one in which the block is missing!

At the front of the frame, just below the barrel, is a knob with a milled edge, locked by a small spring-loaded pin. Depressing the pin allows the knob to be unscrewed, and this permits the sideplate to be lifted off the frame. With the sideplate removed, the left grip can also be lifted away, and the entire working mechanism can be seen. For purposes of cleaning or repair, this a good feature. However, the plate has a groove which is the left rail for the movement of the barrel assembly during recoil, and for the relative high power of the cartridge this is a rather flimsy arrangement.

Aside from the semi-field-stripping described above, further disassembly is definitely *not recommended*. The Glisenti is relatively easy to take completely apart, but the classic phrase "assemble in reverse order" definitely does not apply.

Two types of original grips will be seen—of plain checkered wood, and molded hard rubber with the Italian eagle at center. Those of hard rubber are the most fragile, of course, but whatever the mate-

rial the inside of the left grip is extensively hollowed to clear several parts, and breakage is not unusual. There are no replacement parts of any kind, other than those occasionally found among the used-parts dealers.

The Glisenti is mechanically fascinating, an interesting step in the evolution of the self-loading pistol. As a practical side arm, it was a disaster, and it was soon replaced in Italian service by the Beretta Model 1915.

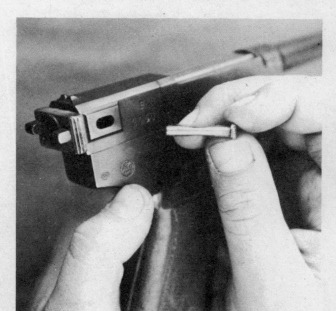

This little cross-bar is the only retainer for the bolt. Fortunately, they are not prone to breakage, as long as low-powered cartridges are used.

Nambu Type 94 Pistol

You have, no doubt, heard stories about this one. The heroic Japanese officer, his troops defeated, takes out his Type 94 pistol, and, with a bow, presents it, butt-first to the victorious American G.I. Suddenly, his hand clenches, and there is the sharp bark of a pistol shot. An 8mm bullet in his heart, the Japanese officer quickly joins his Samurai ancestors.

Stories such as this have resulted in the Type 94 being referred to as the "Surrender Gun." In the above situation the gun was being handled in a fashion whereby the external sear *could* be tripped, with *no* finger on the trigger.

This could have happened; however, it's doubtful it happened with any regularity. First of all, the suicide idea isn't consistent with the code of Hara-Kiri as I understand it. Secondly, the sear of the Nambu Type 94 is rather narrow, and its engagement is *usually* quite stiff. Admittedly, depressing the external sear will trip the hammer; however, on most 94s it is simply *not that easy to push it in with the fingers.*

The Type 94 pistol was designed in 1934 by General Kijiro Nambu, and was originally made at his own factory, intended for commercial export. When WW II came along,

the pistol was adopted for military use, and production was taken over by the Imperial Arsenals. Early examples are well-made and beautifully finished, while those made in late wartime are horrible to behold.

In basic design, the pistol is really not bad. A bit too complicated, perhaps, but it functions properly, and there are no actual weak points in the mechanism. The external sear is pivoted inward at the front, outward at the rear, and the manual safety lever simply covers the rear end of the sear to prevent outward movement, in much the same application as the Luger. The shape of the grip frame may seem strange-looking, but it is oddly comfortable, especially to small hands. The pistol has a pivoting in-

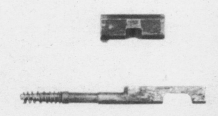

At the top is the breech block key, or retaining bar. Below it is the oddly-shaped firing pin.

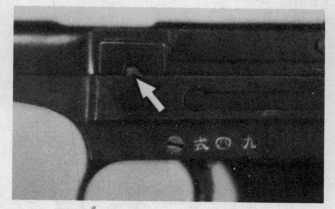

On the Nambu 94 the sides of the locking block should be visible (arrow) in the slide openings on each side.

The two arrows indicate the long external sear—the source of many ridiculous stories.

ternal hammer, and there's a nice design touch at this point—the face of the hammer contains a large roller, to eliminate friction as the hammer is cocked by the recoiling breech block. There is a magazine safety, its easily-seen external arm contacting a recess on the lower back curve of the trigger. The takedown of this gun, even field-stripping, is sufficiently complicated that I do not recommend it for the amateur.

I have seen several references in print that noted with great alarm the fact that the gun can be assembled without the locking block in place and still be fired. This is true, and if you consider only the relatively mild power of the 8mm Nambu cartridge, it's no cause for alarm. There are, however, other considerations. The breech block is a separate unit, contained in the slide and secured by a small, oblong-section cross-key. If this key, or retaining bar, should break, and if the action has not been partially slowed by the unlocking process, the breech block could depart the rear of the slide with considerable velocity. So, assuming you have found a source for custom-made 8mm Nambu rounds and are planning to shoot a Type 94, inspect the small openings on each side of the slide, just above and forward of the trigger. If you can't see the locking block there, don't shoot the gun.

The extractor is tempered to be its own blade-type spring, and most of these are very closely hand-fitted into the breech block. Parts are quite difficult to find, and any that are broken would have to be made. The firing pin is of sufficiently crazy contour that your local gunsmith may mumble a few imprecations before making a replacement. In this case, there is help. The Type 94 firing pin has been commercially reproduced. Considering the scarcity of ammo, I can't imagine why.

Original early grips were of nicely molded hard rubber, later ones were plastic, and very late wartime guns had plain wooden grip panels. The first two named are often found to be chipped or broken, and there are no commercial replacements.

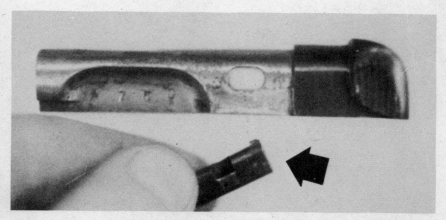

This small oblong-section steel bar is the only retainer for the breech block.

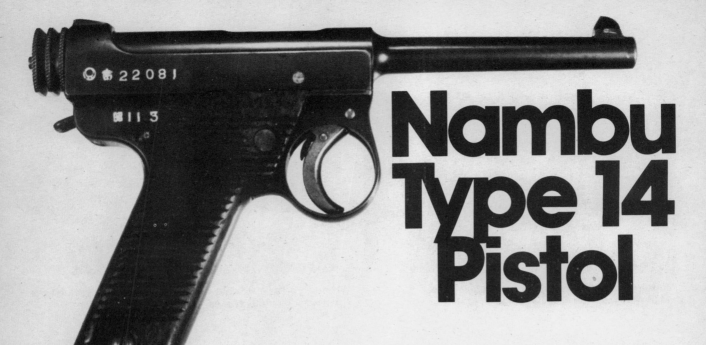

Nambu Type 14 pistol, right side. The frame markings show that this particular gun was made in March of 1936. The small trigger guard is indicative of early production.

Nambu Type 14 Pistol

Because of its odd 8mm cartridge, the Japanese service pistol of WW II is now mostly in the realm of the collector, and that's a pity. It is a well-designed, good shooting gun and never deserved the reputation it once had among gun people who largely dismissed it as junk. It has a trigger system with excellent mechanical advantage, giving it a very smooth pull. It is flat and compact, and the balance in the hand is excellent. Its locking system is stronger than necessary for its mild cartridge and is similar in design to the one used in the Mauser military pistol.

The Nambu cartridge is a bottle-necked round that has ballistics comparable to our .380 auto. The reason for its scarcity is a simple one. In Europe at the end of the war, captured ammo was gathered up and locked in storehouses, reappearing years later on the surplus market. In Japan, storage space was scarce, so the Occupation Authorities decided to destroy the ammo. A sizeable quantity was simply taken offshore and dumped into the ocean. Since the Japanese service pistols were the only ones ever chambered for this 8mm round, it has never been produced commercially in any great quantity. After the war, around 1950,

there was a small company which made excellent 8mm Nambu rounds, but apparently there was not enough interest in shooting the Nambu pistol for production to continue. Custom loaders still produce shootable Nambu cartridges, but most of these use .38 Special brass. It works all right, but the case bodies are undersize, and they swell alarmingly. To make dimensionally perfect 8mm Nambu cartridges, you must start with empty .41 Long Colt cases, and these are almost as scarce as Nambu ammo.

The most undesirable point in the design of the Nambu pistol is the manual safety lever. On the good side, it does directly block the sear. However, there is no stop to prevent its being turned beyond its two lock points on the receiver, and if swung downward from the on-safe position, it will score the grip rather badly. Even when used properly, its long operating lever must be turned upward through a 180-degree arc. This is an awkward movement, and at the top of the arc the thin shank of the lever is unsupported by the receiver. Broken safety levers are a fairly common Nambu ailment.

There is only one flat spring in the Nambu, and this is the extractor, tempered to be its own spring.

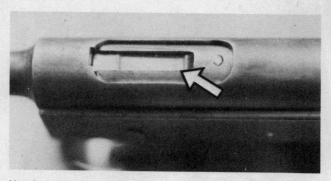

Nambu's top-mounted extractor (arrow) is tempered to be its own spring. Amateur disassembly is usually responsible for breakage of this part.

The long Nambu safety lever is very thin and has no stop to prevent its being turned out beyond its two positions for operation. As a result, it is susceptible to breakage. On the one shown, the lever is broken off next to the pivot.

These do not break often in actual use. Most of those that I've seen broken were the result of amateur disassembly. If you break one, and the used-parts people haven't stripped out an old Nambu lately, then a replacement will have to be made by a gunsmith.

The Nambu is a true hammerless striker-fired pistol, and its striker is unusually long. During its time of production, the striker design was changed, and two different lengths are seen. The striker body and sear beak are well-made and sturdy, but the small firing pin tip does break off with some frequency, especially if the gun is extensively dry-fired. It's not much trouble to replace the point alone, using the original striker body.

The striker spring guide, which not only stabilizes the striker spring but also locks the cocking knob in place, seldom breaks. It is, however, easily lost in careless disassembly. This part looks deceptively simple, but the varied planes of its headpiece must exactly fit the teardrop-shaped aperture in the cocking knob, and it's a fairly difficult part to make. Now, the good news: Triple K has both the spring guide and the striker in currently-made reproductions, and they are not very expensive.

After, "Where can I find ammo?" the next most prevalent question about the Nambu is about deciphering the dating code on the frame. There's an easy formula for this. Japan's Showa period, under Emperor Hirohito, began in the same year this pistol was adopted —1925. The pistol shown in the photos is marked 11.3, which means the 11th year and third month of the Showa reign. Add the 11 to 1925, and the answer is March, 1936.

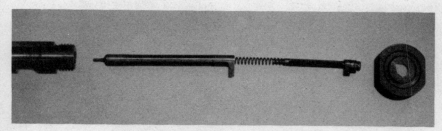

Long striker of the Nambu, shown with its spring and guide, and the detached bolt knob. The striker spring guide is often subject to loss during careless disassembly.

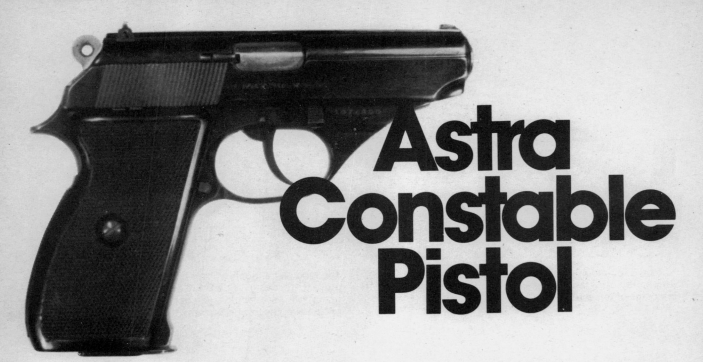

Astra Constable Pistol

The grand old firm of Guernica entered the modern realm of double-action pocket pistols in 1969 with a Walther-looking pistol they designated the Model 5000. It is sold in the U.S. as the Astra Constable and is available in .22 Long Rifle, .32 automatic, and .380 automatic chamberings. While it may externally resemble the Walther pistols, it is entirely different mechanically. The double-action trigger system is closer in design to the Sauer 38H than to the Walther.

The slide stays open when the last shot is fired, and the Constable has something the Walthers lack—an external slide release (a large serrated lever located at the upper corner of the left grip panel). The magazine release is also conveniently located at the lower base of the trigger guard on the left side.

The takedown latch is a spring loaded block of steel with serrated wings on each side of the frame just forward of the trigger. It was reported that in some of the very early pistols there was a problem with cracking of the takedown block, which takes the impact of the recoiling slide. Whether this was due to the design of the block or to the heat treatment of this part, is not clear. In any event, it

was called to the attention of the people at Astra, and the problem was instantly corrected. I have seen no examples of any difficulty, and on the pistol examined and photographed for this section, the part appeared to be practically indestructible.

The safety system of this pistol is like the Walther—up to a point. It rolls two shoulders of solid steel up to shield the firing pin head, also locking the firing pin against forward movement. The last portion of the safety arc also drops the hammer, a less desirable feature. In addition to this, the vertically-moving part on the right side of the frame trips the sear, drops the hammer, locks the slide and also blocks the trigger bar, stopping everything. For those who prefer to do without the hammer-drop feature and want a simple hammer-block safety, this part can be removed without affecting the rest of the mechanism.

This pistol has a full-reach, non-inertia firing pin, and unlike the Walther, it does not have a rebounding hammer. It is unsafe to carry it with a chambered round and the hammer fully down. There is a safety step on the hammer, and it should be used when the chamber is loaded. Once the hammer is

The arrow indicates the takedown latch—an identical serrated wing is on the opposite side of the frame.

set on the safety step, don't operate the manual safety lever, as this will activate the hammer drop and take it off the safety step. If the lever is left in the on-safe position, it's all right, as the firing pin will be shielded. If it's flipped up to off-safe, though, it will leave the hammer fully down, against the firing pin head, with the firing pin point held against the primer of the loaded round. Needless to say, this situation could be hazardous to your health. Just keep the facts above in mind, and the pistol will be quite safe.

The grips are made of a good quality plastic and meet at the rear to form the backstrap of the handle. They are well supported and stabilized, but the right panel is extensively hollowed to accommodate the double-action mechanism and would be susceptible to breakage if struck on the upper part of the side. The back portion of the grips is braced well and better able to withstand impact.

The shooter who owns both the .22 and .380 versions of the Constable has an ideal situation. He can practice economically with the .22 and then feel right at home when carrying the .380 for serious social use. Well-made of quality materials, the Constable is one of the good ones.

This particular part (arrow) serves as a combination hammer drop, slide lock, and trigger bar block; all activated by the slide-mounted safety lever.

Astra Cub Pistols

The Astra Cub shown is the .25 automatic.

The smallest of the Astra automatics is called "Modelo 2000" by the factory, but it was marketed in the U.S. as the "Cub," back in those halcyon pre-1968 days. During the time it was available, though, large numbers of these neat little guns were sold in both the .22 Short and .25 automatic chamberings. In my own younger years when I did a lot more backpacking-style camping, a .22 Astra Cub was an often-carried anti-snake device.

The little pistol is extremely simple, sturdy and well-made, and there is very little that can go wrong, other than an occasional broken firing pin from too much dry-snapping. Owners of these guns, especially the .22, tend to shoot them often and extensively, and I have seen a couple of them in which the disconnector, after many thousands of rounds, was sufficiently worn that the sear and trigger bar engagement had to be recut slightly to compensate.

Both the .22 and the .25 have full-reach, non-inertia firing pins, so carrying them with the chamber loaded and the hammer fully down can be hazardous to your health. A deep safety step on the hammer is provided and should be used when the chamber is loaded. The manual safety lever blocks only the trigger and also serves as a slide latch during disassembly—which, by the way, is very simple and easy.

There is a magazine safety blocking the trigger when the magazine is out of the gun. If the shooter feels that he has sufficient intelligence to remember that there is a round in the chamber when unloading, he can drift out one little pin, shake the safety out the magazine well, and put the pin back. Then, if he's ever in a survival situation and loses the magazine, he still has a single-shot pistol, rather than a useless collection of parts.

The Astra's grips are stabilized against rotation by small integral plugs near their lower edge. These seldom break, but heat-warping can move them out of their recesses in the frame.

The left arrow indicates the round-wire sear spring which seldom weakens or breaks; but, during amateur disassembly it can fly quite a distance. Larger right arrow points to the magazine safety, easily removed by drifting out one pin (small arrow).

The arrow points to the engagement of the trigger bar with the left arm of the sear. After many years of use, disconnector wear may necessitate adjustment here.

The sear spring is a U-shaped piece of round wire in a shallow recess under the right grip panel and is not prone to weakening or breakage. Occasionally, however, some amateur will decide that routine cleaning requires complete disassembly and, after removing the grips, will pry the front arm of this spring out of its notch in the sear arm. At this point, the spring will frequently depart, never to be seen again. Fortunately, they're no trouble to duplicate. Incidentally, all parts for the Cub are still available commercially from several sources.

The grips are the only chronic trouble of this pistol. They were

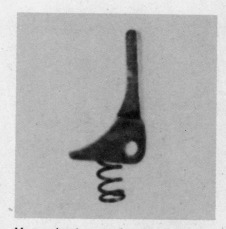

Many shooters prefer that an autoloader *not* be equipped with a magazine safety. The Astra Cub's magazine safety may be easily removed by drifting out one pin.

made of a good quality plastic, but they're very thin and susceptible to warping. Since many of the owners of these little guns tend to keep them in such places as car glove compartments and fishing tackle boxes, in the heat of summer, this shows up fairly often. The grips are stabilized against rotation by molded projections, located near the lower edge, which fit into openings on each side of the grip frame. When they warp enough for these to clear, the grips will rotate. Not only are original-type grips available, but two of the commercial grip-makers offer patterns to fit the Cub.

Astra Model 400 Pistol

One of my esteemed colleagues (Skeeter Skelton, to be exact) has referred to the long-nosed Astra 400 as, "Wart-hog ugly," but I think it has a certain functional beauty. In addition, every part in this design is a little heavier than necessary, properly hardened and made of good quality steel. All springs are round-wire type, and hardly anything ever breaks.

One of the features most often noted is its accidental ability to function with several cartridges other than its original round, the 9mm Bergmann-Bayard or, as it's called in Spain, the 9mm Largo. Many Model 400 pistols will also feed and fire the 9mm Steyr, .38 auto (.38 ACP), and .38 Super. With the first two, this offers a fortunate option. With the .38 Super, it can be dangerous. The Astra is a true blow-back action with no locking system to keep the breech closed during the instant of high pressure. It relies on a heavy slide and a very strong recoil spring, and this is sufficient for the other rounds mentioned. Firing the .38 Super, however, produces violent recoil action which may damage the slide or frame. I've seen a few Astras that had been fired extensively with the .38 Super and had developed hairline cracks in the slide at its narrowest point, below the ejection port. If you shoot a Model 400 and the supply of surplus 9mm Largo or Steyr has run out, use .38 auto, but *not* .38 Super.

Another cartridge to avoid is the 9mm Luger which will function in some Model 400 pistols if certain types of ammo are used. The problem here is that the shorter Parabellum round must rely on the slightly larger diameter of its case body to keep it from going too far into the pistol's long chamber. Some 9mm Luger cartridges—especially U.S. commercial rounds—do not have enough taper or enough rear diameter to "wedge" in the chamber and stay against the breech face. The extractor pushes them in too far, and if the firing pin reaches them, firing occurs with what might be described as an excess of headspace—about $\frac{1}{8}$ of an inch! Even with the European cartridges, which have the necessary "wedging" diameter, it's a risky business. If you want to shoot 9mm Luger in an Astra, look for the shorter Model 600, as it is chambered for that round alone.

Getting back to the .38 auto cartridge (also known as the .38 ACP), some who have tried it in the Model 400 have found that the

A few Astra 400s do not have the bottom-positioned magazine latch. On the Navy type the catch is at the side, as on smaller versions of this design. These guns have the side catch. From top: Navy Model 400 (9mm Bergman-Bayard), Model 600 (9mm Luger) and the Model 300 (9mm Browning Short [.380 ACP]). They are mechanically identical.

slide will not close all the way. The rim diameter of the original 9mm Bergmann round is .392, while the .38 auto measures .405 at the rim. Some pistols have a tightly-machined case head recess in the breech face which will not admit the larger rim. If the gun in question is neither in like-new collector condition, nor one of the rare variations, your gunsmith can use a special long-shank milling tool with a neutral end to open the recess by .013 to accept the .38 auto.

There is one area of chronic damage on the Astra that has nothing to do with its mechanical operation and harms only its appearance. This occurs when someone attempts to "unscrew" the barrel bushing lock with a pair of pliers. The proper procedure, of course, is to depress the barrel bushing with a non-marring tool (a strong thumbnail will do), and the knurled bushing lock may then be easily turned with the fingers. *Caution!* That recoil spring is very powerful and will be released when the bushing lugs are turned into line with the exit channels in the slide. Keep a firm grip on the bushing and lock ring, keep it pointed away from your face and slowly ease out the spring.

As long as you stay with the right cartridges, your Model 400 will never need anything but an occasional cleaning. Mechanically, it's one of the very good ones.

Although many Model 400 pistols will chamber the round, repeated use of .38 Supers can damage the gun. The slide will often crack at its thinnest point (arrow) just below the ejection port.

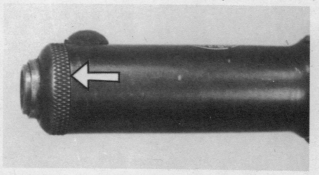

The nicely knurled edge of the barrel bushing (arrow) is often marred through improper attempts at disassembly. Don't use a wrench when a strong thumbnail will do!

Titan .25 Automatic

Imported in some quantity prior to 1968, this little gun was originally designed and made by Tanfoglio Giuseppe Fabbrica d'Armi in Italy. In more recent years all of the parts except the frame are still made by Tanfoglio, then assembled in this country using U.S.-made frames. As presently sold by Excam, the gun is no longer called the Titan but is known as the Targa, Model GT27—it's essentially the same pistol.

The frame and several other parts are of non-ferrous alloy, but the slide, barrel, and most essential parts are of steel. The gun has an external hammer with a safety step, and the safety step should be used, as the firing pin is a full-reach, non-inertia type. The manual safety blocks only the trigger and is also the key to the takedown. With the safety in the on-safe position, the slide can be drawn back beyond its usual limit, lifted up at the rear, and run forward off the frame. This makes for a simple takedown, but it could be interesting if someone, hearing a noise in the night, jacked the slide to load a round in the chamber and had the gun suddenly disassemble. If you keep one of these as a bedside gun, with the chamber empty, be sure to leave the safety lever in the off-safe position, or you could be embarrassed. Or worse.

There are several points in this design that appear to be manufacturing shortcuts and not entirely desirable ones. The ejector, for example, is simply an arm extending upward from the sear. If the ejector breaks, the entire part, including the sear, must be replaced, and this requires that the sear be refitted to the steps on the hammer.

This gun makes no pretense of being a fine piece—it is strictly utilitarian in fit and finish. Even so, some of the mechanical fitting seems to have been done in a rather

During takedown, when the recoil spring unit is removed, the safety lever can fall out and become lost all too easily.

The disconnector (arrow) is an upper arm of the trigger bar. Fitting is rather crude and often must be refitted.

The ejector (arrow) is an integral part of the sear. If the ejector is broken, the entire part must be replaced.

Magazine catch (arrow) is of alloy, not steel. The front lip breaks with some frequency.

haphazard manner. The engagement of the disconnector with the lower edge of the slide, a very important contact, often appears to have been accomplished by touching the part twice to a fast rotary grindstone. On a few I've seen, the work was so crude that the disconnector had to be refitted for proper operation.

I have no quarrel with alloy or even plastic and nylon in modern arms production. Properly used, it keeps down both the price and the weight. In this case, however, there is a classic example of alloy used in the wrong way: The magazine catch is an alloy casting. I have frequently seen these broken in two different locations—at the hole for the pivot pin and at the front lip that retains the magazine. Parts are, of course, available, but that's little comfort if the catch breaks during a serious social encounter. The grips, of thin plastic with a single stabilizing stud on the lower inside edge, are also prone to breakage.

The magazine, on the other hand, is strong and nicely made. A final note: When the gun is disassembled, and the recoil spring unit removed, the safety lever is free to fall out, so be careful it isn't lost.

CZ Model 1945 Pistol

As originally designed by Czech arms genius Frantisek Myska, this little double-action .25 automatic had a manual safety lever on the left side of the frame. This was the Vzor (Model) 1936, and it was not made in large quantity. After WW II, the pistol was very slightly redesigned by Jaroslav Kratchovil, the main differences being the omission of the manual safety and the addition of a simplified magazine safety to prevent firing when the magazine was out of the gun. Both pistols were manufactured by Ceska Zbrojovka, the Model 1936 in the Prague factory, and the later Model 1945 at their facility in Strakonice, Czechoslovakia.

The eliminated manual safety was no loss, as it was really unnecessary on a pistol with a double-action-only firing system. The Model 1945 is not cocked by the action of the slide and requires a full double-action pull on the trigger for each shot. With this feature, it is the ultimate in .25 pocket pistols and is much sought after by both collectors and those who want it for more practical purposes. Unfortunately, our government has decreed that a pistol of this size cannot be imported, so only those that entered the country before 1968 are available, and it's

a rare thing when the owner of one of these lets it go. To rub salt into the wound, the Model 1945 is still being made, and can be purchased in West Germany for the equivalent of around $30.

The Model 1945 is a beautifully designed pistol, and I have repaired these guns very infrequently. They are occasionally susceptible to weakness of the round-wire, torsion-type spring which powers both the trigger return and elevation of the trigger bar unit. This little spring receives rather severe compression in normal operation, and while it seldom breaks, it sometimes loses a portion of its tension. If the pistol is a "shooter," and not a collector piece, I usually drill a hole in the frame, inside, in front of the trigger, and install a coil spring and plunger to power the trigger alone, leaving the torsion spring to tension the trigger bar unit only. This solves the problem.

The trigger bar unit has twin arms which extend to the rear, on each side of the magazine well, to contact the underside of the hammer. These arms are of fairly thin construction, but the high quality of the steel used, and its heat treatment, will usually keep them from breaking. Over the last 30 years, I

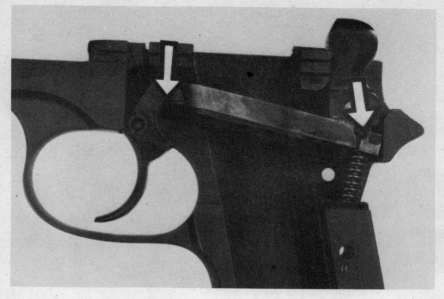

Left arrow points to the combination spring which powers both the trigger return and the trigger bar unit. The right arrow indicates the engagement of the trigger bar arms with the hammer. The bars have been known to break in this area, but this is uncommon.

have repaired exactly two with this ailment. If only one of the arms is broken, the pistol will continue to function for a time, but this puts an unusual strain on the remaining one, and it will eventually let go. In the unlikely event that this happens on your gun, it's best to obtain or make a replacement, although I did repair one by welding thin plates of steel to the broken ends and recutting them to the proper shape.

The grip is a one-piece, wrap-around type, secured by a single screw through the frame. It is made of a good-quality tough plastic, but like most wrap-around grips is susceptible to breakage if the gun is dropped. Fortunately, original-type replacements are available.

The Model 1945 has no other quirks, and its reliability is outstanding. If you find one, buy it, and keep it.

In this field-stripped view, you can see the simplicity of design built into the CZ Model 1945.

CZ Model 1927 Pistol

The resemblance of this gun to the Mauser Model 1910/34 pistols is no accident. The original CZ Model 1922, from which this gun evolved, was based on a prototype designed by Josef Nickl, a prominent Mauser engineer, in 1916. The earlier Czech pistols, chambered for the 9mm Browning Short cartridge (.380 auto), had a semi-locked firing system with a turning-barrel release. The later Model 1927 is a straight blow-back with a non-moving barrel. This pistol was originally a standard sidearm of the Czech military forces, and these early guns will be marked "Ceska Zbrojovka Akc. Spol. v Praze" (Czech Arms Factory, Ltd. in Prague). Those made during the WW II Nazi occupation of Czechoslovakia were marked "Bohmische Waffenfabrik A. G. in Prague" and "Pistole Modell 27 Kal. 7.65," along with the German factory code, "fnh." Pistols made after the Communist takeover will bear the marking "Ceska Zbrojovka Narodni Podnik" (Czech Arms Factory, National Enterprise). The Model 27 was sold commercially in the U.S. by Stoeger for a short time after WW II.

So much for history. Like most Czech arms, the Model 27 is a high-quality pistol of the best materials and workmanship. Even the late war models with a rough external appearance have a degree of reliability that surpasses many other commercial pistols. The Model 27 has few liabilities, and most of these involve the use of old-style flat springs at three points in the design. The hammer spring is a blade-type, and the magazine catch and safety release have tempered shanks, each acting as its own spring. The last two mentioned rarely break, but the hammer spring is considerably flexed in normal operation, and breakage is not unusual. This spring is a simple curved blade with a dovetailed base and a hole for the mounting screw. Making an original-type replacement is not difficult. I have also made successful replacements using doubled round wire. For the parts-replacer, several of the used-parts dealers still have these springs.

During the Nazi occupation, several production shortcuts were employed, and one of these has been known to cause trouble. The firing pin retainer, normally a beautifully machined little tongue-and-groove part, was for a time re-

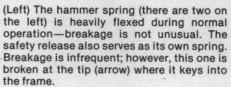

(Right) The CZ27 production was absorbed into Hitler's war machine—this is an early wartime Nazi occupation type.

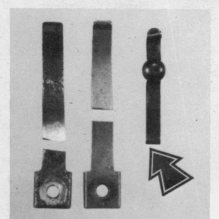

(Left) The hammer spring (there are two on the left) is heavily flexed during normal operation—breakage is not unusual. The safety release also serves as its own spring. Breakage is infrequent; however, this one is broken at the tip (arrow) where it keys into the frame.

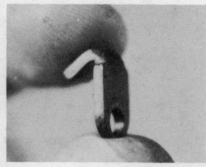

Wartime version of the firing pin retainer was stamped and formed from sheet steel. These have been known to break and should be checked often for cracking.

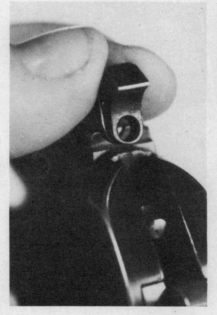

This is the early, fully-machined version of the firing pin retainer—these don't break!

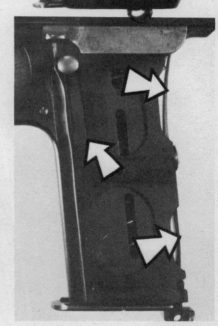

Blade-type springs were used at three points (see arrows) in the Model 27: hammer (top), safety release (middle), and the magazine catch (bottom).

placed by a simple piece of formed sheet steel. I have seen several examples of breakage and heard of one case in which the released firing pin left the slide during recoil with enough force to crack the lens of a pair of shooting glasses. So, if the gun has a stamped-steel retainer, check it frequently for signs of strain.

Early models of this pistol have a very small screw at the lower edge of the sideplate which must be loosened before sliding the plate upward to expose the internal mechanism. The screw is headless with no flange to stop it, and it's possible to over-tighten it and bend the sideplate. When reassembling, be sure to just snug it down gently, then stop.

CZ Model 1924 Pistol

On March 1, 1919 the original Czech Government Small Arms Arsenal was established at Brno, in the province of Moravia, Czechoslovakia. A short time later, engineer Josef Nickl of the famed Mauser Werke in Germany came to Brno to supervise the installation of equipment to produce the Czech Model of the Mauser rifle, and he brought along samples of a pistol he had designed. It was a mating of the basic 1910/14 Mauser Pocket Model with a rotating barrel locking system, with the striker replaced by an external hammer and firing pin. Mauser Werke had made a few prototypes of it, but they were not overly interested. The Czechs liked it, arrangements were made, and the CZ Model 1922 was born. Two years later the people at Prague, now the center for small arms production, redesigned the pistol. They simplified some parts, gave the gun more pleasing lines, and eliminated the gap between the trigger and frame. The result was the Model 1924. Like the earlier gun, it was in the 9mm Short (.380 auto) chambering and had the same locking system.

Some writers in the past have voiced the opinion that for this cartridge a locking system was really unnecessary. It should be remembered, though, that the European loadings of this round were usually somewhat heavier than the standard U.S. commercial level.

The Model 1924 has a manual safety almost identical to the one

There are three blade-type springs used in the CZ's design. The safety lock/release button (left), the hammer spring (upper right) and the magazine catch (lower right).

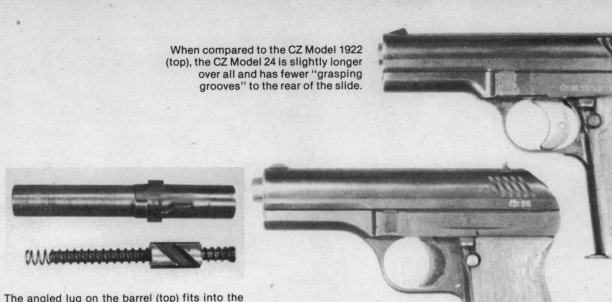

When compared to the CZ Model 1922 (top), the CZ Model 24 is slightly longer over all and has fewer "grasping grooves" to the rear of the slide.

The angled lug on the barrel (top) fits into the matching recess in the lockpiece, shown in its normal position on the recoil spring and guide.

on the Mauser Pocket Pistol with a lever that pulls downward to lock, and a push-button to release it. As in the Mauser, it directly blocks the sear. There is a magazine safety to prevent firing when the magazine is out, and this one you can't remove, as it is also the base for the trigger spring.

There are three flat springs in the design. The safety release button is its own spring and takes all of the strain if some ham-handed type pulls hard on the trigger to "test" the safety. Breakage is not unusual. The magazine catch is also tempered to be its own spring, but this one is heavy and not severly flexed in use. The hammer spring, however, is. This curved blade fractures with some frequency and is also prone to weakening. This spring was commercially reproduced for a time, but I know of no current source for it. I usually replace it with doubled heavy piano wire in a slightly altered shape, and these seem to last indefinitely.

On the left side of the frame, at the top, there is a plate which slides vertically for removal and gives access to the firing mechanism. At the lower edge of this plate is a very small screw which must be loosened before the plate can be

In this rear view of the grip frame, the hammer spring is at the top, the magazine catch spring on the bottom.

The manual safety lever (arrow, upper right) directly blocks the sear. The lock/release button, which is its own blade spring, takes the strain of any hard pull on the trigger at the point indicated by the arrow at the lower left.

After the slide is removed, the sideplate cannot be slid upward until the small screw (arrow) is backed out. When re-assembling, avoid over-tightening of this screw.

moved. When the plate is replaced, don't over-tighten the screw, or the plate could be sprung.

Some of the very late pistols had plastic grip units, but on most of the production this one-piece wrap-around grip was of wood. It is sufficiently heavy and well-supported that breakage is un-usual. It should be noted, though, that modern replacements for the Model 27 pistol are available, and these are adaptable to the Model 1924.

Like most of the Czech pistols of this period, the Model 1924 is out-standing in both materials and workmanship. When you combine its locked-breech design with one of the currently-made high-ve-locity .380 cartridges, you have an excellent home and personal pro-tection pistol.

Mannlicher Model 1901/05 Pistol

Ferdinand Ritter von Mannlicher designed this pistol in 1898, and it attained full production in 1901. It was produced by Waffenfabrik Steyr in Austria, and the manufacturer was hoping for a contract to produce the gun for the Austrian Military. This did not work out, but the pistol was well-liked and was privately bought and carried by many Austrian officers as an unofficial side arm. A medium-sized contract finally materialized, from faraway Argentina, where the pistol was adopted as military standard as the Modelo 1905. Soon after this contract was fulfilled, with no others forthcoming, Steyr discontinued production of the gun. Even so, its popularity in South America and elsewhere kept its odd 7.63mm straight-cased cartridge in production for quite a few years thereafter.

The action of the Model 01/05 is in the retarded blow-back class. In the right slide rail, near the rear of the pistol, there is a small pivoting block on the frame with an upper lug which fits a recess in the lower edge of the slide. This part is tensioned by one end of the large V-shaped mainspring. In initial recoil, the rearward force must first overcome this beveled detent, forcing it downward out of its recess in

the slide. This gives a moment of hesitation during the instant of high pressure—in effect a semi-locked system.

These pistols are outstanding examples of Austrian gunmaking of the old school. The fit and finish of all parts is superb, and producing a gun of this design and quality would be virtually impossible today. When sold as military surplus by Argentina, these pistols, by government order, had the Argentine crest ground away on the right side of the frame cover, and the guns were then arsenal reblued, but even this did not hide the evidence of meticulous hand-fitting by Steyr.

As one would expect in a pistol design of this era, blade-type springs are prevalent. Not only are these more likely to break or weaken, but the shape of them is decidedly weird, and in two cases includes an integral mounting stud. The hammer spring, as previously noted, is a massive V- type, located on the right side of the frame. One

The Mannlicher Model 1901 pistol shown is the Argentine contract type of 1905.

Arrow points to the original heavy V-blade spring that powers the hammer and slide retarding block. Note the hook-like projection that contacts the hammer.

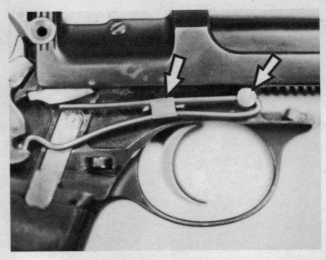

A modern replacement of the mainspring, using heavy round wire, a cross-drilled boss to fit the stud recess, and a spacer (left arrow) to maintain tension.

In spite of the fragile appearance of the thin tempered tail of the extractor (arrow), this part seldom breaks.

end bears on the little slide friction block, and the other has a hook-like projection which contacts the right wing of the saddle-shaped hammer. On the left side of the frame, a smaller V–shaped blade spring powers the trigger, sear and disconnector. Don't ask me to explain how a single V-blade powers three parts—we don't have that much space in this section. Let's just observe that von Mannlicher was a genius and leave it at that. Both of the springs described above are mounted on the frame by lateral studs which are part of the springs, and to make an exact replacement for a broken original would be an interesting, and expensive, endeavor.

If the owner doesn't mind having a modern touch hidden behind the frame cover plates, it is possible to replace both of these springs with braced piano wire, utilizing the stud holes as seats for fitted bosses having transverse holes for the wire. The photos above show how this can be accomplished. It works perfectly, but if von Mannlicher could see it, we'd probably hear a few pungent Teutonic expletives.

The top-mounted extractor has a tempered tail and acts as its own spring. The tail is fairly thin, but I have observed no cases of breakage. This is probably due in part to the quality of the steel and its treatment by the artisans at Steyr, and in part to the fact that no flexing is required in installation as the extractor is retained by a cross-screw. Incidentally, the screw-loop of the extractor also retains the firing pin, and it should be noted that the firing pin is a full-reach, non-inertia type. So, when carrying this gun with the chamber loaded and the hammer down, the little hammer-block safety on the right rear of the slide should be flipped back and down to keep the hammer from touching the firing pin head.

The location of the safety lever may cause some to wonder, why put it on the right side of the pistol? Because, *meine Herren,* in those days, the pistol was for the left hand, the saber for the right, *nicht wahr?*

There is really nothing else in the Model 01/05 that is susceptible to damage, but perhaps it should be noted that when the frame cover is off the gun, its thin sideplates should be handled with care, as they are fitted rather precisely to the frame. Original grips are of vertically-grooved wood, well-mated to the grip frame, and breakage is rare. Of course, re-

Mounting stud (arrow) of a V-blade spring which powers the trigger, sear and disconnector.

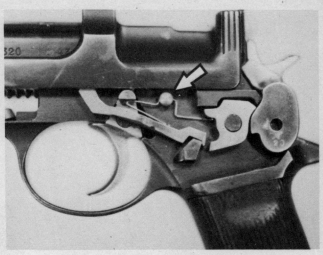

Arrow points to a cross-drilled boss fitting the stud recess and holding a round-wire spring that replaces a broken original. Note that the shape of the spring is not the same.

placements for anything broken will be totally unobtainable.

There is one quirk in the design which should be explained, as it often baffles those unfamiliar with this pistol. The slide locks open when empty, and most people, knowing this is a gun loaded from the top with strip-clips, will push down the magazine follower, expecting the slide to run forward. When it doesn't, they wonder what to do next. The answer is to pull downward on the hammer. The open slide is caught not only by the magazine follower but also by the same little block that retards the slide movement in the firing cycle. Pulling the hammer downward brings the hook on its spring against the tail of the locking block, turning it out of engagement with its notch in the slide.

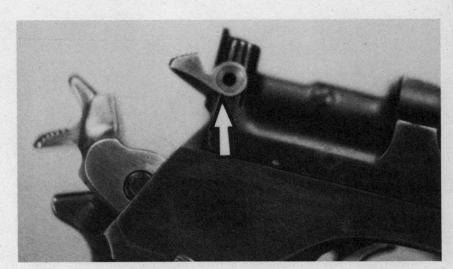

The hammer-block safety (arrow) is located on the right rear wing of the slide.

Mann .25

In 1919, Fritz and Otto Mann designed one of the most weird-looking little .25 pistols ever made. It was produced between 1920 and 1923 at the Fritz Mann Werkzeug-fabrik in Suhl-Neundorf, Germany, and fewer than 20,000 of these guns were made. It may be that its strange appearance contributed to its short production span. It has also been said that the lower edge of the cocking piece on its internal breech block would pinch the hand, but I don't think this has much validity. I have fired the Mann pistol, and the knob comes nowhere near the hand, being placed high at the rear of the frame with a long, sweeping curve below it.

In spite of its odd shape, there

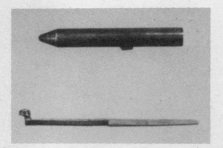

The unusual Mann striker (top), with its conical firing pin point. The combination ejector and safety-lever detent (bottom) is thin and fragile.

are several interesting points in the design of the Mann. Its tapered upper frame makes it very flat and concealable. By slightly retracting the bolt and turning the exposed knurled portion of the barrel, the barrel is easily removed for cleaning. The magazine release is a push-button, set into a recess in the frontstrap of the grip frame. The manual safety is a simple trigger-block type and locks into the on-safe position by snapping over a stud which is also the mounting post of the ejector. In a feature echoed many years later in the Hi-Standard pistols, the trigger bar and sear area is covered by a thin steel plate set in a shallow recess and retained by the left grip panel.

There have been several .22, .25, and .32 automatics made entirely without extractors, relying on blow-back and the low case adhesion of these calibers to get the empty out. The little Mann, though, is in a class by itself on this point. It has no separate extractor, but there is a fixed flange of extractor shape on the forward end of the breech block—an integral part. As the cartridge rises from the magazine, its rim slides under this extractor-flange. This is, in effect, a fixed extractor, and the first round can be loaded only from the

Automatic

The extractor flange on the front face of the breech block is rugged—it seldom breaks.

magazine—it can't be dropped into the chamber through the ejection port. One good thing about this "extractor"—it's not likely to break, as it's a heavy part of the breech block.

Anchored by the safety-catch stud mentioned above, the ejector is also held in position inside the frame by a groove in the breech block. The ejector is a long, slim part and is easily broken. Usually, it will snap off near its retaining stud. The sear is powered by a flat spring which has a retaining hole at its upper end that fits over a pin on the sear. Unlike the ejector, it would be fairly simple to reproduce.

The Mann is a true hammerless, striker-fired pistol, and the striker point is of unusual design. Instead of being stepped down to a small-diameter firing pin at the forward end, the point of the Mann striker is conical and is not likely to break. The grips are molded hard rubber, retained by a single screw on each

side, and the right one is well-supported by the frame. The left one, however, is unsupported at its lower edge and subject to frequent breakage. There are no ready-made replacements. In fact, for a limited-production piece like the Mann, any parts needed will have to be made by a gunsmith.

As mentioned above, removal of the barrel is simple and easy. Further takedown, however, is not recommended for the non-gunsmith. The process is sufficiently

complicated and tricky that the amateur may be tempted at several points to use force, and the result will be breakage of unobtainable parts.

After the demise of the little .25 pistol, Mann went on to produce a larger pistol of more conventional design in 7.65mm and 9mm Kurz (.32 and .380 auto), and about 20,000 of these were made between 1924 and 1928. All of the Mann pistols are of more interest to the collector than the shooter.

In the area indicated by the arrow, a thin steel plate covers the trigger bar and its engagement point with the sear. With grip removed, the plate can easily be lost.

MAB Model PA-15 Pistol

Since 1921, the Manufacture d'Armes de Bayonne has been making a varied line of good automatic pistols. The designs were not startling, being mostly of typical Browning pattern with a few original touches. Then, in 1967, they introduced a new pistol for the 9mm Luger cartridge, and it is outstanding in several ways. The two most obvious departures from the usual are the magazine and the locking system. The magazine tops by one round the capacity of the Canadian version of the Browning Hi-Power, holding 15 rounds. The locking system was a variation of the one used by Roth and Krnka in the Roth-Steyr and Steyr-Hahn pistols, a turning barrel governed by a lug running in a track inside the slide. One of the advantages of this system is its ability to function with a wide range of loads of varying pressures, an area where conventional locking systems give occasional difficulty.

The pistol was an outgrowth of an experimental MAB gun called the Modele R, and the new gun was designated the Pistolet Automatique 15, a reference to its capacious magazine. An otherwise identical pistol with a straight-line, eight-round magazine was also made, called the PA-8. The Model

The barrel and heavy recoil spring base are shown in proper engagement. Note the beveled lug on top of the barrel, which engages a track in the slide for rotation.

PA-15 is a heavy gun, weighing 39.15 ounces empty. It is all machined steel, having only two internal stamped parts—the trigger bar/disconnector and the magazine safety. Even the floorplate of the magazine is machined from a flat block of steel! This thing sits in your hand like the Rock of Gibraltar, and missing the target almost has to be intentional.

The slide latch is long enough for good leverage and extends back into the top front corner of the left grip for easy reach with the thumb. The safety is also well-located at the rear and directly blocks the sear. The firing pin is a full-reach, non-inertia type, and the safety step on the hammer should definitely be used when carrying with a loaded chamber.

There is only one flat spring in the design. This one powers the sear and is not severely flexed in normal operation. The pistol has a magazine safety, making it impossible to fire with the magazine removed, and this one is more aggravating than most of them. It directly blocks the sear, and with the hammer down and the maga-

A special spanner-type tool for disassembly of the PA-15's magazine catch (arrow) is required. Note the well positioned slide latch and safety.

zine removed, the slide cannot be opened, as the blocked sear will bind on the hammer. Fortunately, this little abomination is easily removed, along with its spring and plunger, without otherwise affecting the operation of the pistol.

Original grips are of good quality plastic, secured by a single screw on each side and are well-supported by the frame. Breakage is unlikely. Replacement parts of any kind may be a problem, though such routine things as a firing pin could be easily made by a gunsmith. These guns were imported for a short time by a dealer in Chicago, but for several years now there has been no importer of the MAB line. In the unlikely event that any major part should fail, you might have to write directly to the factory in Bayonne, France.

Nevertheless, this is one of the very good ones.

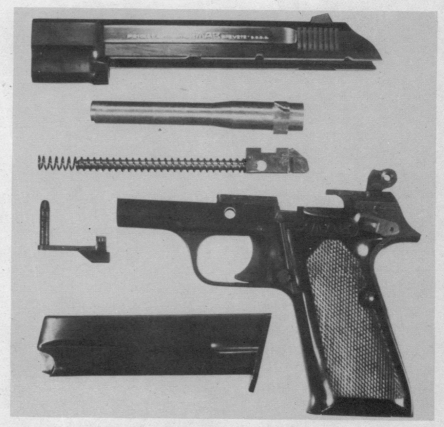

As massive as the PA-15 is, it is a snap to field-strip. It's reliable, accurate and a fistful of fire power.

Lahti Pistol

Both the Swedes and Finns made the "Lahti" pistol. This Lahti is the Swedish Model L-40 as made by Husqvarna Vapenfabriks.

This pistol was designed by Aimo Johannes Lahti, director of the Valtion Kivääri Tehdas (State Rifle Factory) in Jyväskyla, Finland, and adopted as military standard by Finland in 1935. In 1940, a somewhat modified version was adopted by Sweden for its military forces, and manufacturing rights were licensed to the Husqvarna Vapenfabriks in Sweden. Since the internal design of the Swedish and Finnish models is not radically different, there is no need to go into the changes here.

Externally, the Lahti pistol has the look of a massive Luger. The takedown lever, safety lever, and stock lug are also similar, but there the resemblance ends. Instead of the Luger's Maxim-toggle arrangement, Lahti used a variation of the locking system of the Bergmann-Bayard, and the square-bodied bolt is also in this pattern. The Luger is striker-fired, while the Lahti has a pivoting hammer concealed in the frame. On the Swedish model, the recoil spring is a captive unit which stays on the frame when the pistol is field-stripped.

One design point which sets the Lahti apart from other pistols is the presence of a feature usually found only on machine guns—an accelerator. The Lahti was made for use in a climate where snow, ice and extreme cold are a major consideration in military operations. At very low temperatures, thickened oil and retarded ignition can cause ejection problems. To offset this, Lahti added a small pivoting

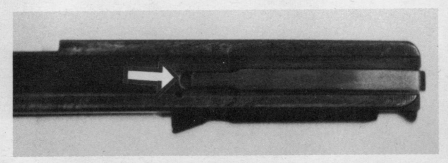

Like some autos, the extractor on the Lahti (arrow) is tempered to be its own spring, but this is a heavy part and does not often break.

Note that the takedown lever (arrow) is similar to the one on the Luger and operates much in the same way. This is the Swedish pistol.

When removing the left grip panel, the safety lever (arrow) must be sprung over its stop pin and rotated out to the rear.

lever at the forward lower edge of the barrel extension. At the instant that the rear movement of the extension unlocks the bolt, the lower arm of the accelerator strikes a shoulder in the frame, causing its upper arm to deliver a sharp rap to the forward edge of the bolt. Regardless of weather conditions or weakened ammo, that bolt will open with alacrity. A word of caution, though, to Lahti owners in more temperate climes who use their pistols frequently: To avoid damage, especially when using heavier loadings, the accelerator should be removed and kept in a safe place (in case the Ice Age returns). To remove it, rotate the part until the small hole lines up with the spring-powered retaining pin. Insert a small-diameter tool (an unfolded paper clip is perfect) in the hole to depress the pin, and lift out the accelerator. The retaining pin and spring can now be removed, and they are quite small, so be careful they aren't lost.

The extractor is tempered to be its own spring, but these are fairly heavy, and breakage is rare. The grips are of good quality plastic and are supported well by the frame. The left grip, however, is often broken by amateur attempts at removal. Before taking it off, it

The accelerator (arrow) is located at the forward lower left edge of the barrel extension. The gun shown is the Swedish model.

On the Swedish model, the recoil spring and guide are a captive unit on the frame.

Extensive firing in a warm climate has caused a hairline crack in the barrel extension near the accelerator. If the accelerator is removed (and it can be) cracking will be eliminated.

is necessary to spring the safety lever over its stop pin and turn it beyond its usual position to clear the grip. In this operation, you must also be very careful to spring the tempered safety lever just far enough to clear the pin, and no further, or it can break off. If at all possible, just leave the grip in place, and don't bother it.

The Finnish models of the pistol are still in use as military standard in that country, and these are scarce in the U.S., bringing respectable collector prices when they turn up. Sweden changed to the Walther P-38 a few years ago, and a number of the Swedish Lahti pistols have seen sold as surplus in the U.S. These, too, have gradually disappeared into collections. It's a shame there aren't more of them around, as the pistol is beautifully made of the best materials and extremely accurate.

Along with the surplus pistols that were sold in the U.S., a large stock of parts came over, and these were purchased by several dealers. So, if something routine should break, such as a firing pin, parts are available.

Luger Pistol

Typical commercial Luger in 7.65mm. The one shown is the 1920 type.

In a book of this type, there is no need to go into the fascinating lore of the Luger. For the arms student or collector, its myriad variations are well-covered in full-length books by Datig, Jones, Kenyon and Reese. Before examining its mechanical details, I think we should note that around the world it has various names. In Germany, it was known earlier as the "Pistole 08," in reference to its year of adoption by the military. "Parabellum" is another of its titles, and in 1923 the Stoeger Company registered the name "Luger" for U.S. commercial sales. In this country, the latter designation is the one most used, whether the pistol in question was commercially sold or brought home by a returning soldier.

The collecting of Lugers has reached such proportions that any piece with all numbers matching, even a common 1920 commercial pistol, is almost too valuable to shoot. Fortunately, there are still a few mismatched pistols around for those who recognize it as a fine shooter's gun. Its grip and balance have been copied by many others over the years, but none of these ever captured the exact "feel" of the Luger. Incidentally, it is possible, in spite of the multi-direc-tional linkage involved, to give the pistol an excellent trigger pull.

As with many of the older designs, the Luger has blade-type springs powering many of the parts. In very early guns, prior to 1908, the extractor and recoil spring were of this type, but pistols of this vintage are in the realm of the collector. On the ones likely to be encountered, flat springs power the sear, magazine catch, hold-open device, ejector and safety lever, the last two being tempered to serve as their own springs. In normal operation, these are not prone to breakage. They are not flexed to their limits in use, and the quality of tempering, even in war-time models, is consistently high. In fact, most of the breakage I've seen was the result of amateur disassembly and reassembly. This especially applies to the ejector which should never be removed unless absolutely necessary, and then it must be done very carefully by someone who knows the right way.

In spite of its relatively intricate mechanism, the Luger is not prone to breakage of parts. This can be partly credited to good design with ample allowance for strength, and partly to the use of the best quality steel, heat-treated to exactly the

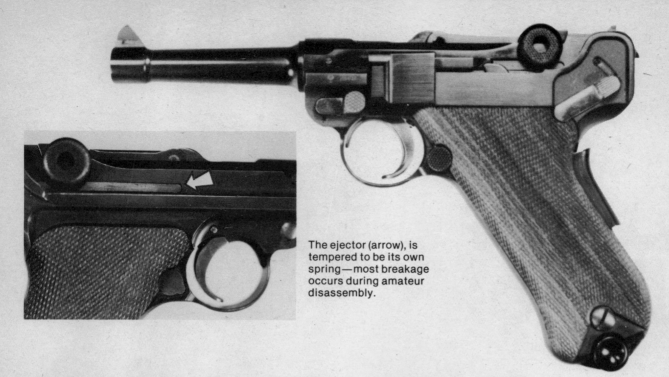

The ejector (arrow), is tempered to be its own spring—most breakage occurs during amateur disassembly.

A beautiful recreation of the Pistole 08 by Mauser/Interarms, this one in 9mm was made in 1973.

The flat spring (arrow) which powers the hold-open device is easily broken during disassembly or reassembly.

right hardness for each component. Even when there are no broken springs or parts, though, you still hear frequent complaints of jamming, and this is easily explained. There are no bad Lugers —just uninformed shooters.

When a Luger malfunctions, jamming on feed or ejection or failing to feed at all, the trouble is almost always due to one of three factors, or a combination of these: low-powered ammunition, a worn or deformed magazine or a weak magazine spring. The toggle-type locking system of this pistol is extremely efficient, and cartridges must have sufficient power to operate the action. The absolute minimum for proper operation seems to be around 1,200 foot-seconds in velocity, and the standard U.S. commercial load is somewhat below this level. A few years ago, there was an ample supply of surplus Canadian and European ammo that had the necessary power, but most of this is now gone. The handloader or those who buy custom loads will have no problem tailoring rounds to suit the Luger. For those who can only buy off-the-shelf U.S. commercial loadings, there is one easy answer: Have your gunsmith remove about one to two coils from the recoil

spring of your gun, and assuming one of the other two factors are not present, the domestic stuff should work fine thereafter.

The excellent grip angle of the Luger, which gives the pistol its fine handling qualities, also results in a magazine system that is very sensitive to wear and the tension of the spring. Bent or deformed feed lips will be fairly obvious and, if serious enough, may require replacement of the magazine. Fortunately, these are available from several sources, and you can usually get the late-pattern Swiss or German magazines which are much better and stronger. A less obvious ailment is wear at the top edge of the catch aperture on the magazine —the hole in the upper right front curve where the catch enters. The catch is very hard and seldom wears. The milder sheet steel of the magazine does, and wear at the point mentioned can cause the magazine to sit low in the grip frame. As little as one or two millimeters of drop can cause misfeeding. Sometimes, this syndrome is caused not by wear, but by the

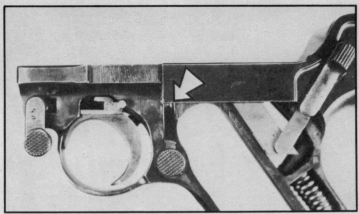

When the blade-type magazine catch spring breaks, reproduction is made difficult by the formed locking hump (arrow) at its upper end.

In a "mismatched" Luger, the rear of the cocking arm can strike the indicated rear upper edge (arrow) of its recess. In extreme cases this can result in the fracture of this entire section.

The arrow indicates the upper edge of the catch aperture on the magazine where wear can cause misfeeding.

magazine being not original to the gun. To check for this, with an *empty* magazine in the gun, push upward on the bottom of the magazine endpiece (and don't be misled by a loose endpiece). If the magazine can be moved into the gun quite a bit from its position as held by the catch, you probably have a problem. If you have a number of otherwise good magazines on hand, you might consider having your gunsmith add a tiny spot of weld to the catch, recutting and fitting until all of the magazines are held snugly in place. A weak magazine spring can also cause misfeeding, and here the cure is simple—just replace the spring.

There is one other quirk of the Luger which should be mentioned, as it is especially seen in the mismatched shooter types. On the left side of the breech block at the forward section of the toggle assembly, there is an opening, a recess, for the retractor arm on the middle section to engage the cocking lug on the striker (firing pin). During recoil, the arm draws the striker back to cocked position. If the parts are not perfectly matched, the rear face of the arm can strike the rear upper edge of its recess, sometimes with enough force to

break off the entire left upper rear edge of the breech block. In view of this, it might be well to check the clearance at this point, as replacement breech blocks for the Luger are not particularly abundant.

In fact, all Luger parts are in short supply. Some of the used-parts dealers have a few, from time to time, and such things as the striker have been commercially made. For any major part, your best chance is probably custom-Luger-maker John V. Martz, whose address you'll find in the Parts Suppliers Directory in the back of this book.

Stoeger .22 Luger Pistol

Gary Wilhelm, who was also responsible for the Model 71 Plainfield pistol, designed this gun for Stoeger Arms Corporation. The Stoeger company registered the use of the name "Luger" back in 1923, when they were importing the genuine article from Germany. When the new .22 pistols appeared on the market about seven years ago, they were marked "Luger." Judged on the basis of coming close to the feel and balance of the original German pistol, they deserve the "Luger" marking. In actual mechanical detail, though, the only relation is the toggle-joint breech system. Internally, Wilhelm used an entirely modern approach with a "package" firing mechanism—a sub-frame containing most of the working parts. All springs are round-wire type, either helical coil or torsion action with ample weakening allowance.

The main frame and some other parts of the pistol are of high-tensile-strength alloy, and in all applications the dimensions are sufficient to preclude any breakage. The barrel liner and operating parts are steel, and some of the parts in the firing system are stampings. The trigger pull is excellent. Unlike the original Luger, which was striker-fired, the Stoeger pistol has a pivoting internal hammer, and a light, crisp trigger pull. The manual safety, located in the same place as on the original, directly blocks the sear.

During the few years this pistol has been on the market, I have had occasion to repair only one, and that case could not really be called a repair. When the gun is taken apart, and the firing system removed, it is possible to turn the safety beyond its normal arc. When this is done—and it was, in the case mentioned—the safety positioning plunger and its spring can depart with startling speed, and because of their small size, finding them is unlikely. My only

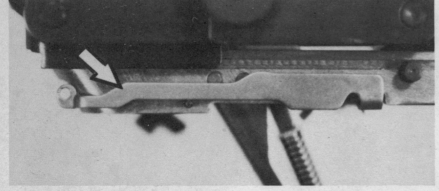

While the sub-frame is out of the receiver, the trigger bar (arrow) is easily disengaged from the unit—its not easily reinstalled.

Arrow indicates the screw which maintains the engagement of the trigger and trigger bar. Removal of this screw is one of the steps in the takedown procedure.

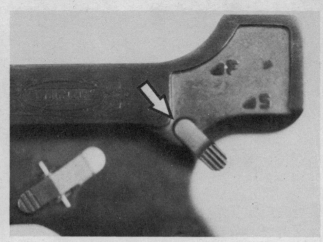

With the sub-frame removed, the safety lever (arrow) can be turned beyond its normal arc. Don't turn it to the position shown, or the positioning plunger and spring may be released to fly out.

"repair" was to replace these missing parts. I have seen no cases of broken parts, jamming, or any other malfunction.

Although the takedown of this pistol is not difficult, reassembly can be quite tricky, and I recommend you leave that thorough, once-a-year cleaning to your friendly gunsmith. Replacing the firing system in the frame is easy, and putting back the large pin that holds the lower extension of the unit is not too difficult. The tricky part is reattaching the trigger bar to its stud on the trigger, which must be done through a small access hole on the left side of the frame. Once you have managed this, you must be sure it doesn't slip off the stud while replacing the screw which closes the hole and holds the loop of the trigger bar on the stud. If this sounds complicated, rest assured that for the non-gunsmith, it is.

The screw that closes the access hole is the only point on which I am certain I can criticize this otherwise excellent gun. On earlier examples of this pistol, this screw was made of either steel or alloy. On the one shown in the photos, the screw was *plastic!* This, I think, is carrying the modern concept of manufacturing too far. If

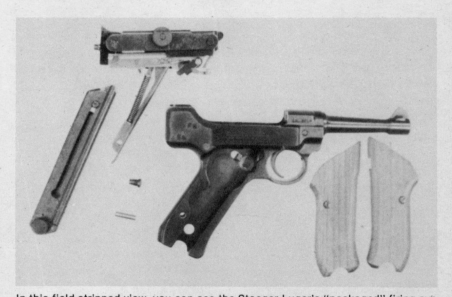

In this field-stripped view, you can see the Stoeger Luger's "packaged" firing system in the upper left. Disassembly beyond this point is *not* recommended.

only slightly over-tightened, the plastic threads will strip. If you drop this screw on a shag rug or in the tall grass, you can't find it with a magnet. When I get one of these guns, and I think I will because I like it, the first thing I will do is duplicate that little plastic screw in good steel.

The original grips are of real wood and nicely checkered. They are well supported by the frame, and breakage is unlikely. Parts

breakage is also unlikely, as they are designed for strength. The extractor, for example, is large and heavy for a .22 pistol. Except for the tricky takedown and reassembly, and that plastic screw, this is a good one.

The trigger bar holding screw, one key to the takedown procedure, is currently made of plastic. Note the two stripped threads near the blank tip.

Manufacturers and Importers

Some of the firms listed have been in business for many years, and have also produced several of the older guns listed in the book. Parts for these long-discontinued arms were exhausted many years ago. Trying to obtain them from the manufacturer will waste a lot of time—both yours and theirs. In this case it's best to go directly to the used or surplus parts dealers. When you do write the parts folks be sure to mark your letter, "Attention: Parts Department." For the older parts, check the listing of used-parts dealers in this book.

In regard to the older guns, some of the manufacturers can supply certain information, such as when a particular gun left the factory, where it was shipped, the original finish and so on. A small research fee is usually charged for this service.

Bauer Firearms
34750 Klein Avenue
Fraser, MI 48026

Beretta Arms Company
P. O. Box 697
Ridgefield, CT 06877

Browning Arms Company
Route 4—Box 624-B
Arnold, MO 63010

Clerke Products
2219 Main Street
Santa Monica, CA 90405

Colt Firearms
150 Huyshope Avenue
Hartford, CT 06102

Connecticut Valley Arms
Saybrook Road
Haddam, CT 06438

Excam, Inc.
4480 East 11th Avenue
P.O. Box 3483
Hialeah, FL 33013

Garcia Sporting Arms Corp.
329 Alfred Avenue
Teaneck, NJ 07666

Harrington & Richardson
Industrial Rowe
Gardner, MA 01440

High Standard Mfg. Co.
31 Prestige Park Circle
E. Hartford, CT 06108

Interarms, Ltd.
10 Prince Street
Alexandria, VA 22313

Iver Johnson
Fitchburg, MA 01420

Plainfield Ordnance Co.
P. O. Box 251
Middlesex, NJ 08846

Raven Arms Company
Baldwin Park, CA 91706

Remington Arms Company
Bridgeport, CT 06602

Savage Arms Corporation
Westfield, MA 01085

Smith & Wesson, Inc.
2100 Roosevelt Avenue
Springfield, MA 01101

Sterling Arms Corp.
4436 Prospect Street
Gasport, NY 14067

Stoeger Arms Company
55 Ruta Court
S. Hackensack, NJ 07606

Sturm, Ruger & Company
Southport, CT 06490

TDE Marketing Corp. (OMC)
11658 McBean Drive
El Monte, CA 91732

Parts Suppliers Directory

Numrich Arms Corporation *(A general dealer)*
West Hurley, NY 12491

Sarco, Incorporated *(Surplus military & general parts)*
192 Central Avenue
Stirling, NJ 07980

Martin B. Retting *(A general dealer, some older*
11029 Washington Blvd. *parts)*
Culver City, CA 90230

Sherwood Distributors *(Surplus military & general parts,*
18714 Parthenia Street *also currently reproduced parts)*
Northridge, CA 91324

Triple K Mfg. Company *(Replacement magazines &*
568 Sixth Avenue *reproduced parts, some surplus)*
San Diego, CA 92101

Fenwick's Gun Annex *(A general dealer)*
P. O. Box 38
White Hall, MD 21161

Traders Den *(A general dealer)*
1011 Excelsior Ave. W.
Hopkins, MN 55343

Ozzie's Gun Parts *(A general dealer)*
P. O. Box 274
Mineral, IL 61344

Bob's Gun Shop *(A general dealer, specializing in*
P. O. Box 2332 *parts for modern imported guns)*
Hot Springs, AR 71901

David H. Granger *(Early revolver parts, especially*
9412 N. Oakleaf *Smith & Wesson)*
Tampa, FL 33612

Military Parts Specialists *(As the title implies, esp. Mauser*
P. O. Box 35033 *M/96, etc.)*
Houston, TX 77035

John V. Martz *(Luger parts)*
8060 Lakeview Lane
Lincoln, CA 95648

Dixie Gun Works *(Primarily for muzzleloaders, but*
Gunpowder Lane *many parts for early cartridge guns*
Union City, TN 38261 *as well)*

Mrs. C. H. Weisz *(Same category as Dixie, also*
P. O. Box 311-N *reproduction grips for many*
Arlington, VA 22210 *cartridge handguns)*

Index